COOKING WITH
Kosher
THE ʌBUTCHER'S WIFE

Dedicated to the memory of my beloved father Edwin Smith, who loved his meat,
and my father-in-law Shmuel Lurie, who really knew his meat!

AUTHOR'S ACKNOWLEDGEMENTS

Thanking people is always the most difficult part of any project completed, not because it's hard to say thank you, not because you may forget somebody, but because everyone you've come into contact with during your life, whether good or bad, has had some hand in bringing you to where you are today. However, there are a few people who do stand out with regard to this book.

To my soul mate and incredible husband Ian and our four very precious and special gifts, Baruch, Darren, Ryan and Eden. You are the very essence of my being, the ones who have given me the tools to create this book, and for that I thank you.

To the most unbelievably creative photographer in town, Michael Smith (who just happens to be my brother too!), thank you for allowing me to peep into your professional world of photography, an experience I shall never forget. You are a whizz kid, but didn't we always know that?

To my 'creative team' Rod, Graham, Steph and Lauren (brothers and sisters too!), your invaluable support gave me the faith to transcend all limitations – may the laughter linger on forever! To my sister-in-law Brenda, who physically pushed me into the publishers office – look where I am a year later!

Finally to my mother and mother-in-law, Nanna Jill and Bobba Roch, your unconditional love and encouragement have allowed me to follow a path in life I never thought I could.

The author and publishers would like to thank the following for the loan of their homeware products: Monsoon, Gently Worn, Mad about House, Classy Junk, Rustic Rose, Congo Joe, Lucky Fish, Grand and Grotty, @home, Die Ossewa and La Grange.

First published in 2006 by Struik Publishers (a division of New Holland Publishing (South Africa) (Pty) Ltd)
New Holland Publishing is a member of Johnnic Communications Ltd
Cornelis Struik House, 80 McKenzie Street, Cape Town 8001
86–88 Edgware Road, London, W2 2EA, United Kingdom
14 Aquatic Drive, Frenchs Forest, NSW 2086, Australia
218 Lake Road, Northcote, Auckland, New Zealand

www.struik.co.za

PUBLISHING MANAGER: Linda de Villiers
MANAGING EDITOR: Cecilia Barfield
EDITOR: Irma van Wyk
DESIGNER: Beverley Dodd
PHOTOGRAPHER: the redhead's studio – Michael Smith
STYLISTS: Natalie Bell, Annaleze Behr and Lauren Weiner
PROOFREADER AND INDEXER: Joy Clack

Reproduction by Hirt & Carter Cape (Pty) Ltd
Printed and bound by Craft (Pte) Ltd, Singapore

ISBN 1 77007 296 9 (9 781770 072961)

10 9 8 7 6 5 4 3 2 1

www.imagesofafrica.co.za

IMAGES OF AFRICA
PHOTO LIBRARY

Over 40 000 unique African images available to purchase from our image bank at www.imagesofafrica.co.za

CONTENTS

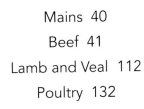

INTRODUCTION

So … you thought that being 'the butcher's wife' would mean an endless supply of the best cuts of meat – wrong! It's that same old story, the shoemaker goes without shoes … you know the rest.

The first lesson I learnt, marrying into a fourth-generation family of butchers, was that the popular kosher cuts such as Scotch fillet, lamb chops and veal schnitzel would never make it onto our table. These were *'for the customers'* and it was not negotiable. So if it wasn't one of the popular cuts it either landed up on our table or it was made into 'polony'!

After 25 years of experimenting, creating and improvising, I feel confident enough to finally dispel the old myth that because we can only eat from the forequarter we are limited to tough, dry and boring meat! Kosher meat is of the highest grade and quality and hopefully with the notes, tips and recipes in this book, you'll never have to be nervous about 'trying something new'.

This book contains a collection of the 'thumbs up' recipes from the most critical bunch around (sons and brothers can be rather harsh) and any previous misconceptions about kosher meat will finally be *'shechted'* (slaughtered)!

Cooking with kosher meat doesn't mean we can't be creative. Lamb shanks don't have to be burnt offerings on a Seder plate and poor ol' beef shin doesn't have to be a piece of meat bobbing around in a soup pot. It, too, can be uplifted to its full potential as Italian osso buco. Whether it's meaty bones, mince or brisket, each and every cut on the forequarter has its own unique flavour and texture and there is most certainly 'life after Scotch fillet'!

Cooking with kosher meat is no different from cooking with any other meat. If it's French cuisine you fancy, or tantalising Thai you're trying, making it with kosher meat should be no different. With the ever-increasing kosher products and non-dairy alternatives continually being added to the list of ingredients, we just don't have any more excuses. Almost every kosher caterer in South Africa and elsewhere in the world is able to keep up with the times by offering every type of cuisine imaginable at their functions.

This recipe book contains only meat (fleischik) and non-dairy (parev) recipes. There are a few reasons for this. The dietary laws of keeping kosher forbids the eating of dairy products and meat together. A six-hour period should elapse before dairy can be eaten after meat. Therefore, all desserts, after eating a meat meal, may not contain any milk or dairy products whatsoever.

Most of my family are lactose intolerant (allergic to milk and dairy products) and this, together with a couple of other allergies conveniently thrown in, makes meat and non-dairy products the only option in our home. And as for fish … well, my children believe fish look better in ponds than on plates! Besides which I married a butcher and not a fishmonger!

My friend Liora always said: 'God knew what He was doing when He gave you a butcher for a husband – if my family had all these eating problems they would have lived on apples!'

So, with all this in mind and the convenience of being a butcher's wife with a 'limited' supply of meat, was there ever an option anyway?

A BIT ABOUT KOSHER …

Kosher is not a cooking style but rather a lifestyle.

The life of a Jewish person is supposed to be governed by Torah Law, yet most husbands beg to differ, feeling theirs is governed by their mothers-in-law!

Although they may have a positive effect on our health – the dietary laws, of course – it's a fallacy that they are based on health or hygiene. We adhere to them purely because we are told to. This affirmation of faith provides a diet for the soul as well as for the body. I suppose your mother-in-law could lay claim to that too!

There are many areas of concern in the field of Kashrut, but for the purposes of this book we will be dealing mainly with meat recipes and, because of the prohibitions of mixing milk and meat together, the non-dairy substitutes where applicable.

OK, so let's start exploring the forequarter ….

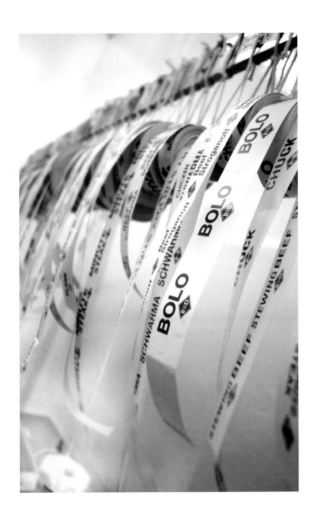

OVEN TEMPERATURES

CELSIUS (C)	FAHRENHEIT (F)	GAS MARK
100 °C	200 °F	¼
110 °C	225 °F	¼
120 °C	250 °F	½
140 °C	275 °F	1
150 °C	300 °F	2
160 °C	325 °F	3
180 °C	350 °F	4
190 °C	375 °F	5
200 °C	400 °F	6
220 °C	425 °F	7
230 °C	450 °F	8
240 °C	475 °F	9

CONVERSION TABLE

METRIC	US CUPS	IMPERIAL
5 ml	1 tsp	³⁄₁₆th fl oz
15 ml	1 Tbsp	½ fl oz
60 ml	4 Tbsp (¼ cup)	2 fl oz
80 ml	⅓ cup	2¾ fl oz
125 ml	½ cup	4½ fl oz
160 ml	⅔ cup	5½ fl oz
200 ml	¾ cup	7 fl oz
250 ml	1 cup	9 fl oz

THE DIFFERENT KOSHER CUTS

LET'S PLAY WITH THE FOREQUARTER

Who says we were dealt the lousy hand? Who says the inferior cuts are on the forequarter? There's no downside to any cut on the forequarter as the same nutrients are available from both ends of the animal. OK, so we can't change the hand we were dealt but we can certainly change the way we play it. Let's raise the odds, take the pot and start cooking! Remember, the steaks don't have to be high, just tender!

THE FOREQUARTER OF BEEF

Most beef cuts are made up of muscle tissue and, as we know from gym, the more a muscle is used the stronger/tougher it becomes. Frequently used muscles like in the leg and shoulder, need to be cooked over a longer period, either by braising (browning the meat first then adding a little liquid and cooking it for a long time) or boiling. Cuts such as top rib and Scotch fillet are not exercised as much, so before their personal trainers get wind of this, dry roasting is still the best method of cooking them.

Besides being delicious, meat has a high nutritional value and no other food group is as good a source of protein. Understanding the different cuts of beef can be confusing. Not only do they have different names in different countries, but the butcher around the corner will call his cut by a different name too!

The forequarter is divided into the chuck, rib, fore shank, brisket and plate. The most economical way of buying beef, lamb or veal is purchasing the whole forequarter and having your butcher cut it into the various cuts to suit your needs.

CHUCK SECTION

The chuck section comes from the shoulder and neck of the animal and yields some of the most flavoursome cuts of meat.

Neck

Although very tasty, the meat in the neck is made up mostly of connective tissue, bone and fat. It can either be cubed, minced or used in your stockpot.

Hump

This boneless piece of meat is probably the most forgotten cut on the forequarter. More often than not, when a recipe calls for brisket, I use hump because it's leaner. It really pickles well and is also good for hot beef on rye!

Chuck roast/square roast/cross-rib roast

This contains the meaty portions on the top of the first few ribs and consists of several muscle layers running in different directions. So you thought only we were confused – so is the poor animal! This makes a wonderful pot roast or moist, slow-cooked oven roast.

Raisin-rib roast

This is a chuck roast off the bone. It makes a delicious, tender roast that benefits from slow, wet cooking methods like stewing, braising or pot-roasting.

London broil

Now this is an interesting cut, which some say isn't actually a formal cut, but rather a method of preparation! However, this is the cut that has been commonly accepted as 'London broil'. I call it 'forever loyal' because it is always soft and tender.

Shoulder bolo

This is a very lean roast, off the bone, used by most butchers to make rare roast beef for their deli section. Most chefs would say that this heavily exercised muscle should be braised or cooked in liquid, however if dry roasted and thinly sliced, it makes a wonderful rare roast.

Round bolo/mock tender

If wet aged (vacuum packed in the fridge) for seven to ten days this makes a delicious roast for three or four people. It's a small, very lean cut that can also be used for minute steaks and stroganoff, or cubed for stews, steak pies and curries. It really is a very versatile cut. One of my favourites!

Side bolo steak/oyster steak/
boneless blade steak

This is a small but tender cut of meat that can be sliced vertically and cooked as steaks or cubed for kebabs/sosaties. This is quite a thick piece of meat – about 3–4 cm thick – so when ordering it, I order it as a whole piece and cut it in half horizontally through the middle following the white sinew line so that each steak is now only 1.5–2 cm thick. This way you don't have the sinew running through the middle of the steak or meat.

An oyster steak is cut with the line of sinew running through it as it is cut vertically not horizontally.

Blade steak/seven-bone steak/
American beef chop

This steak has a bone in it and makes a very tender, tasty variation to a lamb chop (for those who prefer beef). It gets its name from the bone, which is shaped like the number seven.

RIB SECTION

One thing that breaks my heart is when customers request roasts with 'no fat'. The meat should rather be roasted with the fat on to keep it moist, tasty and succulent, then if it hasn't all rendered, removed afterwards!

Standing rib roast or prime rib roast

It is in this section of the ribs that the tender Scotch fillet or rib-eye muscle is housed. While still attached to the rib bones it is called a standing rib roast and makes a wonderful impression as it stands arched firmly on its flat-boned base. This roast can also be French-trimmed, where all the meat and fat are removed along the length of the bone tips for that extra-clean look.

Scotch fillet or rib-eye roast

The rib-eye muscle or meat removed from these ribs is known as the Scotch fillet or rib-eye roast. It is a boneless roast that can be roasted whole or cut into Scotch fillet or rib-eye steaks. The steaks cut on the bone are known as T-bones.

Beef ribs

The ribs from which the Scotch fillet is removed are used to make those lovely marinated or smoked steakhouse ribs or they can be cut shorter.

Top-rib roast

This is one of my favourite cuts of meat. It is rather a small rib roast (should feed about four people) with a thick layer of lean beef that can easily be carved on or off the bone. I use this sliced, for my tzimmes, rather than brisket.

FORE SHANK/SHIN

This wonderful piece of meat, when crosscut into slices, makes the best osso buco in town. It houses the famous marrowbones, which are delicious in soups and stews. The collagen in the meat turns to a soft gelatine while cooking, which keeps the meat soft and tender. It makes delicious soup meat as well and, once cooked, can be minced for your 'perogen' (page 24).

BRISKET

This is a boneless, rather fatty roast (see why I like hump!) from the breast of the cow. This cut is usually pickled and boiled for hours to be used in one of its famous dishes as 'hot beef on rye' or 'corned beef' as some prefer to call it. Apparently it got the name 'corned beef' because the Irish practice was to cure it with corn-sized grains of salt – probably like our koshering salt! It also makes wonderful deli pastrami and smoked brisket cold cuts.

ROLL OF BEEF

A roll of beef is normally a piece of brisket rolled, tied and roasted with string to keep its shape. However, any flat piece of meat can be rolled for roasting, including deboned lamb or veal.

PLATE/FLANK

This small area, limited because we only go up to the tenth rib, contains some ribs and flank which is wonderful for cholent and stews. The rest of the meat in this area is used for mince, polonies and sausages.

THE FOREQUARTER OF LAMB
Neck

As oxtail isn't kosher, I had to find the next best thing. After experimenting with a few cuts this was definitely it! Neck is very tasty and tender, and somehow absorbs all the flavour of the spices in which it is cooked, making it a wonderful alternative for curry.

Shoulder

This tasty roast can be served on the bone or deboned and rolled. It can be cut as a 'raised shoulder', which is the meaty blade without the chops (feeds 4–6 people), or as is normally the case, cut with the chops and shank bone (feeds 8–10).

Rack of Lamb

Single lamb chops are cut from this rack; double lamb chops are closer to the shoulder. A rack makes an elegant roast, but unfortunately doesn't serve too many. If the meat is stripped along the length of the bone tips, it's called a French rack. It's a lovely roast for two hungry people to share on a special occasion. When ordering, tell your butcher how many chops you want on the rack. There are normally about five or six.

Shank

The word shank reminds me of something we have on our Seder plate at Pesach time. However, the lamb shanks I'm referring to here are lean, meaty, larger and very tasty, and for this reason alone have become extremely popular. I quite often add a couple of shanks or breasts to the roasting pan if I feel a shoulder won't be enough. There it goes again, that hereditary disease I've inherited that I may 'run short', G-d forbid!

Breast

Breast of lamb must be one of the most versatile cuts around. It can be roasted, braaied/barbecued, stewed, stuffed, smoked, cooked whole or even cut up into single ribs or 'ribbetjies'.

'For true tenderness, nothing beats a well-aged hunk!'

MARINADES
bastes and rubs

MARINATING MEAT
all the tips, all the secrets and much, much more …

Marinades are tasty, seasoned liquids that enrich the flavour as well as break down the fibres in meat. This tenderising process is aided by the use of an acid in the marinade. Acids such as lemon juice, vinegar, wine and beer help to soften the tissue of tougher meat cuts. Natural tenderising ingredients are those found in fruits such as pineapple, ginger and papaya. Papaya is an unbelievable tenderiser, so much so that I placed a steak in between some mashed papaya to see if it really was what they made it out to be and the next morning I had stringy, mushy, mincy, meaty 'something'!

Most of the marinades we buy in supermarkets today are both marinades and basting sauces in one, which enables us to marinate and cook the meat in the same sauce.

Some recipes call for you to marinate the meat first, then to discard the marinade and apply a basting sauce or rub. I sometimes do this if I haven't allowed the meat to tenderise in a vacuum bag for long enough and need it urgently. I will therefore marinate it overnight in something with a high acid content, rinse it the next day to remove the acidic taste (as the acid content will be too high and cause the meat to taste bitter), then leave it to sit the whole day in a basting sauce. The basting sauce enhances the flavour and colour of the meat and prevents it from drying out.

Marinade that has been in contact with raw meat should not be poured **cold** over already-cooked meat. You can safely use it during the cooking process because it will boil through. If you must re-baste your meat, rather pour fresh basting sauce that hasn't had raw meat in it into a bowl and paint it on the meat just before removing it from the braai/barbecue.

Never take meat, that is cooked, off the braai/barbecue and give it a 'last dip' in the marinade. Remember this marinade has had raw meat in it and is a 'no-no' from a health point of view!

Vacuum-packed meats from your butchery that are already marinated don't have to be re-marinated. They are normally a combination of a basting and marinating sauce and the meat can be cooked in the sauce. It can be removed from the bag and put straight into the oven, in a pan or on the fire.

Always marinate meat in the fridge and never at room temperature.

Marinate in a glass dish/bowl or a zip-lock bag, or leave the meat in the vacuum bag containing the marinade from a butchery. Do not use an aluminium bowl as it could react with the acid in the marinade and give the meat a metallic taste.

Ensure that the meat is completely immersed in the marinade – if not, turn the meat occasionally during the marinating process so that all the sides are equally exposed to the marinade.

THE BUTCHER'S BASTER
no. 1

'STEAKOUTS' ARE NEVER PLANNED IN OUR HOME BUT WHEN THE CRAVING GETS TO US, THOSE STEAKS HAD BETTER BE SOFT ENOUGH FOR A THREE-TOOTHED COWBOY TO CHEW ON! TO MAXIMISE THEIR TENDERNESS, GET THEM VACUUM PACKED AND KEEP THEM IN THE FRIDGE FOR 10 DAYS (I DO IT FOR TWO WEEKS), THEN FREEZE THEM.

¼ cup Worcestershire sauce
½ cup red wine
½ cup tomato sauce
2 Tbsp molasses
½ cup chutney (mild to hot, whichever you prefer)
2 Tbsp brown vinegar
½ cup brown sugar
1 Tbsp ginger syrup
1 tsp freshly crushed/chopped garlic
1 tsp mustard powder

Combine all the ingredients in a glass jar. Make sure the lid fits tightly and shake it up well. Place in the fridge until needed – it keeps very well.

When you're ready to fry or braai/barbecue your steaks, pour a bit of the basting sauce into a bowl and either dip each steak in the sauce just before frying or paint each steak with basting sauce while it's cooking.

MAKES ±3 CUPS

THE BUTCHER'S BASTER
no. 2

BASTER NO. 2 CONTAINS NO WINE BUT HAS THE SUBTLE FLAVOUR OF COFFEE. SO, DEPENDING ON WHO YOU'RE ENTERTAINING, IT'S EITHER THE WINE TO MAKE THEM YAWN OR THE COFFEE TO KEEP THEM UP TILL DAWN!

½ cup black coffee (1 tsp strong coffee powder in ½ cup hot water)
½ cup tomato sauce
¼ cup Worcestershire sauce
¼ cup brown sugar
1 Tbsp ginger syrup
1 tsp freshly crushed garlic
1 tsp mustard powder
¾ cup hot chutney
1 tsp hot chilli sauce

Combine all the ingredients. Dip the steaks into the basting sauce or brush them with sauce while cooking.

MAKES ±3 CUPS

MARINADES, BASTES AND RUBS

my favourite
TENDERISING MARINADE

DID YOU FORGET TO AGE YOUR STEAKS AND NEED THEM FOR SUPPER? THEN TRY THIS TENDERISING SHORTCUT!

2 tsp crushed garlic
2 tsp grated ginger
¼ cup soy sauce
¼ cup Worcestershire sauce
1 cup red wine
½ cup brown vinegar
½ cup molasses
1 cup tomato cocktail juice
½ cup brown sugar
½ cup oil
1 tsp mustard powder

Blend all the ingredients together with a hand blender or in a food processor or liquidiser.

MAKES ±4 CUPS

Notes: This marinade should not be confused with a basting sauce. The acid in the vinegar, wine and tomato juice acts as a tenderising agent. Its liquid consistency is necessary for easier absorption. The steaks should be placed side by side in a glass dish and covered with the marinade. They shouldn't marinate for longer than 6 hours. Remove the steaks, shake off any excess marinade and braai/barbecue or fry the meat. Further basting in a basting sauce is not necessary as there is enough flavouring in the marinade.

MONKEY GLAND
sauce

THE BEST GLAND IN THE LAND!

1 heaped cup chopped onions
little oil for frying
1 heaped tsp freshly crushed garlic
1 cup chopped ripe tomatoes
(1 drained can is also fine)
1 cup grated green apple
1 cup tomato sauce
1 cup chutney (I prefer hot)
½ cup Worcestershire sauce
½ cup red wine
1 cup loosely packed soft brown sugar

Fry the onions in the oil just until they start turning golden brown.
   Add the garlic, tomatoes and grated apple. Fry until soft, then add the rest of the ingredients. Simmer for about 30 minutes.
   When cool, blend either in a food processor or with an electric hand blender.

MAKES 6–8 CUPS

COFFEE
marinade

DON'T WORRY, THIS WON'T KEEP YOU UP ALL NIGHT!

2 cups chopped onions
1 tsp crushed garlic
little oil for frying
1 heaped tsp coffee powder,
dissolved in 1 cup hot water
½ cup Worcestershire sauce
1 cup tomato sauce
½ cup brown sugar
3 Tbsp peri-peri sauce

Fry the onions and garlic in the oil. Add the rest of the ingredients and simmer for 20 minutes. Blend until smooth.

MAKES ±4 CUPS

always
COCA-COLA® MARINADE

THEY'VE ALWAYS SAID THAT 'THINGS GO BETTER WITH COKE®' SO WHY SHOULD STEAK OR CHICKEN BE ANY DIFFERENT? HOPEFULLY THIS MARINADE WILL BE 'THE REAL THING®' FOR YOU BECAUSE IT'S DEFINITELY A CASE OF 'COKE® IS IT'!

1 large onion, chopped
little oil for frying
1 tsp crushed garlic
1 cup tomato sauce
1 cup Coca-Cola®
(or Coke Light®)
2 Tbsp Worcestershire sauce
1 tsp mustard powder
2 Tbsp wine or brown vinegar
salt and pepper

Fry the onion in the oil until lightly browned. Add the garlic and fry for another minute or two.
Add the remaining ingredients.
Simmer on low heat for 20 minutes.
When cool, blend until smooth with a hand blender, or in a liquidiser or food processor.

MAKES ±2 CUPS

MARINADES, BASTES AND RUBS

AROMATHERAPY OIL
for shoulder roasts

DON'T WE ALL LOVE AN AROMATHERAPY SHOULDER MASSAGE? SO WHY SHOULDN'T LAMB AND BEEF EXPERIENCE A HERB OIL RUB?

½ cup loosely packed chopped parsley
2 tsp koshering salt
1 tsp crushed peppercorns
3 long sprigs of rosemary (pull leaves off sprigs)
6 sprigs of thyme (pull thyme off stalks)
12–14 basil leaves
1 cup olive oil
2 Tbsp lemon juice
1 onion, quartered
3 cloves garlic
½ cup red wine

Blend all the ingredients with a hand blender, in a liquidiser or food processor. Take a handful or two of the herb oil and rub it over the entire shoulder roast.

MAKES 2 CUPS

PERI-PERI
sauce

THIS IS A MUST IN EVERY FRIDGE. IT DOESN'T LAST TOO LONG IN OUR HOME AS WE LOVE SPICY FOOD, BUT IN MOST PEOPLE'S HOMES IT LASTS FOR ABOUT A YEAR!

¼ cup tiny, red hot chillies, stems cut off, sliced in half and seeded
6 cloves garlic (garlic lovers can add more!)
1 Tbsp treacle sugar (sticky soft brown sugar)
1 Tbsp brown vinegar
1 cup olive oil

Blend all the ingredients with a hand blender, in a liquidiser or food processor. Store in a glass jar with a good sealing lid.

Note: I know the chillies need to be cut in half to be checked for insects, but I've always wondered which insect would have the 'chutzpah' to try and live in a hot chilli! Maybe that's why I never find them alive!

MAKES ±1 CUP

MARINADES, BASTES AND RUBS

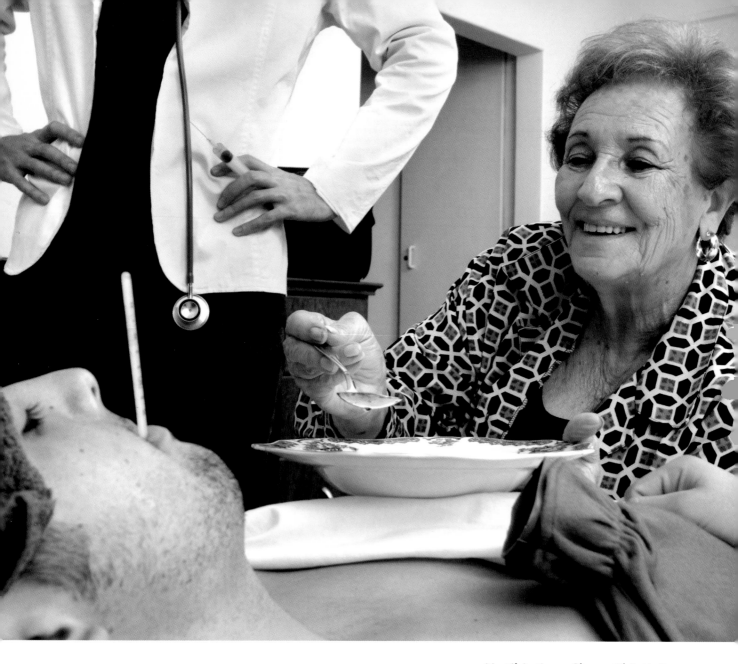

'Antibiotic … Shmantibiotic!'

LIQUID
assets

Russian
CABBAGE AND POTATO SOUP

WHEN I HEAR 'RUSSIAN SOUP' THE FIRST THING THAT COMES TO MIND IS BORSCHT OR SWEET-AND-SOUR CABBAGE SOUP WITH LITTLE MEATBALLS. HOWEVER, THIS RECIPE IS ONLY CALLED RUSSIAN CABBAGE AND POTATO SOUP BECAUSE IT HAS RUSSIAN SAUSAGE IN IT!

2 Tbsp oil
6 Russian sausages, sliced in half lengthwise then chopped
2 cloves garlic, crushed
2 large onions, chopped
3 large leeks, chopped
6 potatoes, peeled and diced (smaller rather than bigger)
3 x 250 g packets coleslaw mix (ready-cut shredded cabbage and carrot)
4 Tbsp chicken stock powder dissolved in 2.5 litres boiling water
salt and pepper

Heat the oil in a large soup pot. Add the Russian sausages and fry for a few minutes until golden brown (not too dark or they will become too hard and crispy). Remove and set aside.

To the same soup pot, add the garlic, onions and leeks, and continue frying until the vegetables become limp. Add the potatoes, coleslaw mix and chicken stock, and bring to the boil. Reduce the heat and leave the soup to simmer for at least another 2–3 hours. Add salt and pepper to taste.

Place a hand blender in the soup and pulse it a couple of times – this brings it all together! Just before serving, add the sausage and bring to the boil.

Serve with rye bread.

SERVES 8–10

disguised DOUBLE CORN SOUP

I WAS RAISED ON CHICKEN SOUP, BUT WHEN I SAY CHICKEN SOUP I MEAN CHICKEN SOUP! EVERY SINGLE PART OF THAT CHICKEN WAS USED! TO THIS DAY, THE MINUTE I FEEL SLIGHTLY UNDER THE WEATHER MY BODY CRIES OUT FOR IT. IS THERE A BETTER ANTIBIOTIC? I MAKE THIS WHEN MY CHILDREN ARE AT SCHOOL, BECAUSE IF THEY SAW 'FISELACH' (FEET) AND CHICKEN CARCASSES BOBBING AROUND IN A SOUP POT THERE'S NO WAY THEY'D EAT IT. I MEAN, WHO PUTS 'CHICKEN' INTO CHICKEN SOUP? SO TO ENSURE THEY GET THEIR DOSE OF MEDICINE, I HAVE TO DISGUISE IT AND THIS IS HOW IT'S DONE!

5 chicken carcasses

1 x 250 g packet chicken feet

1 x 250 g packet chicken necks

1 x 250 g packet chicken stomachs

3 whole carrots, peeled

1 large onion

2 sticks celery

4 litres water

3 chicken stock cubes

1 tsp salt

2 cups frozen corn

1 x 410 g tin cream-style sweetcorn

2 Tbsp cornflour

Wash the chicken pieces well. Place a large soup pot onto the stove. Spray the inside with olive oil and fry the chicken until golden brown. The bottom of the pot should go slightly brown in places.

Add the carrots, onion and celery and continue frying for about 10 minutes, stirring every now and then.

Add the water, chicken stock cubes and salt, and bring to the boil. Reduce the heat and simmer (with the lid lying loosely on the top) for about 2 hours. The liquid should reduce by a quarter.

Strain the soup through a muslin cloth or fine strainer. Leave the soup to cool and skim the fat off the top (placing the soup in the freezer will help the fat to harden – it can then be lifted off easily). At this point you have a hearty chicken stock or soup.

Once the fat has been removed, scoop one cup of cooled chicken soup from the pot and set it aside in a glass bowl. Place the rest of the soup back on the stove, add the corn and sweetcorn, and bring it to the boil.

Meanwhile dissolve the cornflour in the cup of cooled chicken soup and add it to the hot soup, stirring quickly as you do so otherwise it could go lumpy. Once it starts to thicken, turn off the heat, cover the pot and leave it to stand.

Notes: By the time the children get home, the evidence has been removed and they think it's corn soup. If they only knew the healing power of each mouthful! Here's to all our children's health, always!

SERVES 8–10

PEROGEN
loaf

WE'VE HEARD OF THE LOAF VERSION OF GEFILTE FISH. WELL, THIS IS THE LOAF VERSION OF 'PEROGEN' (MINI SOUP MEAT PIES).

2 onions, chopped
1 carrot, chopped or grated
little oil for frying
500 g mince meat
salt and pepper
1 x 400 g roll puff pastry
1 egg and 2 Tbsp water, beaten,
to be used as an egg wash

Fry the onions and carrot in a little oil until brown. Remove from the pan and set aside. Add a little more oil to the pan and fry the mince until cooked through and slightly browned (this gives the perogen filling a nice taste).

Add the mince to the onion and carrot mixture and mix well. Add salt and pepper to taste. At this point you have two options – either place all the ingredients into a food processor and pulse it a couple of times to 'bring the mixture together', making it a little smoother, or you could run the mixture through your mincer once, mixing it well with a spoon after it has been minced.

Open out the pastry and cut it in half lengthwise. Lightly roll out each piece of pastry on a flat, floured surface. Don't roll it out too thinly! Spoon the meat filling all the way down the centre of the length of the pastry. Dip your fingers into a little water and press the meat filling into a thickish sausage shape.

Fold both sides of the pastry towards the centre over the meat and seal it by firmly pressing it together with your fingers. Carefully lift the loaf onto a well-greased baking tray, paint it with egg wash and bake at 180 °C until golden brown. Repeat with the other piece of pastry. If you don't need both loaves, freeze the other raw one until needed, then bake.

Slice and serve in soup.

Notes: It's important to remember that the pastry should be a long rectangular piece because the loaf is not rolled up like a Swiss roll. Rolling the perogen loaf like a Swiss roll makes the loaf too doughy on the inside as the pastry only becomes crisp on the outside.
The pastry should meet in the middle just as you would make small perogen.

SERVES 6–8

DURBAN CURRIED SOUP
with a tropical hint

MY HUSBAND ALWAYS FELT THAT THERE HAD TO BE SOME CULINARY BENEFITS TO MY BEING RAISED IN DURBAN. SURELY A GOOD 'DURBAN CURRY' WENT WITH THE TERRITORY? MINE SEEMED TO BE DOING THE TRICK QUITE WELL, UNTIL MY BROTHER MARRIED NORTH COAST'S VERY OWN 'CURRY QUEEN'. MY SISTER-IN-LAW STEPH BELIEVES THAT THIS TITLE BELONGS TO HER MOTHER, BUT AS FAR AS I'M CONCERNED THE ROYAL LINEAGE CAN GO AS FAR BACK AS THEY WANT IT TO, AS LONG AS THEY GIVE ME THE RECIPES!

2 skinless chicken breasts, on the bone
2 Tbsp peri-peri oil
2 onions, chopped
½ tsp crushed garlic
1 heaped tsp medium curry powder
1 ripe banana, chopped and mashed slightly
2 Tbsp finely chopped fresh coriander
1 x 410 g tin curried vegetables
1 x 410 g tin mild chakalaka
2 litres water
1 cup coconut milk
salt and pepper
coriander leaves for garnishing

In a large soup pot, fry the chicken breasts in the peri-peri oil until golden brown. Remove from the pot and set aside. (Don't worry if it's not completely cooked through – it will cook through later.)

In the same pot, fry the onions and garlic (you may need to add a little more oil). Add the curry powder, banana, coriander, tinned vegetables, chakalaka and water.

Return the fried chicken pieces to the soup pot, bring to the boil, then reduce the heat and simmer for at least 1½–2 hours.

Remove the chicken from the soup, remove the bones and chop the meat into very small pieces. Place the meat back into the pot.

Finally add the coconut milk, stirring as you add it, and salt and pepper to taste. Simmer for another 20 minutes. At this point, if you feel the soup is too thick, add a little more water with a little chicken stock powder. Garnish each serving with a coriander leaf or two.

Notes: There are so many things that determine the thickness and liquidity of soups. The size of the soup pot can make a big difference! A large pot makes the liquid evaporate a lot quicker and one person's simmering point may be another person's boiling point!

SERVES 8–10

BEAN, BARLEY AND BILTONG
soup

AS A SOUP LOVER, THIS IS ONE OF MY FAVOURITE WINTER MEALS! SO WHEN YOU CAN'T PULL YOUR FAMILY AWAY FROM THE TV SET BECAUSE SOUTH AFRICA IS PLAYING WHATEVER AGAINST WHOMEVER, YOU MAY AS WELL JOIN THEM IN THEIR PATRIOTISM AND GIVE THEM HOME-GROWN BILTONG SOUP! WHAT COULD BE BETTER?

½ cup small white beans
1 cup butter beans
1 cup barley
2 bay leaves
5 large carrots
4 sticks celery
2 onions
3 large leeks
oil for frying
2 slices meaty shin
4 large potatoes, peeled and cubed
3 litres chicken stock (home-made or 3 chicken stock cubes to 3 litres water)
salt and pepper
250 g shredded biltong

Wash the beans and barley and place in a large bowl with the bay leaves. Pour over boiling water and leave it to stand overnight or for at least 3 hours. Make sure the beans and barley are covered with plenty of water as they absorb quite a bit.

Chop and slice the carrots, celery, onions and leeks. Pour a little oil in the bottom of a large soup pot and fry the meat to seal it. Add the vegetables (except the potatoes) and fry for a few minutes, stirring continuously.

Drain the beans and barley and discard the bay leaves. Add the cubed potatoes, beans, barley and chicken stock to the soup pot and boil for approximately 2 hours. You may need to add a little more water at this point if you feel the soup is too thick. Some beans retain more water than others. Why should they be different from us?

Add salt and pepper to taste, and leave the soup to simmer for at least another 2 hours on low heat.

When serving, sprinkle a tablespoon of biltong over each bowl of soup.

Notes: After boiling the soup for the first 2 hours, you could transfer it to a crock-pot and continue cooking it there. I prefer doing it this way so that I don't have to keep checking on it. In fact, I leave mine to cook on low for 6–8 hours.

If you're cooking it on the stove, once the beans are soft, switch off the heat and leave it to stand for 30–45 minutes just to relax and absorb the flavour, then either refrigerate or reheat the soup when ready to serve.

SERVES 8–10

CREAMY CHICKEN AND ASPARAGUS SOUP
with whole wheat crumbles

TRADITIONALLY, CREAMY ASPARAGUS SOUP WAS ALWAYS SOMETHING WE ATE WITH A MILK MEAL, QUITE SIMPLY BECAUSE IT WAS MADE WITH MILK AND THICK DAIRY CREAM. WELL, HERE IT IS, NOT ONLY THICK AND 'CREAMY', BUT WITH MEAT TOO!

3 chicken breasts, on the bone
2 onions, chopped
little oil for frying
3 litres cold water
3 x 450 g tins white asparagus pieces
3 Tbsp cornflour
2 Tbsp asparagus soup powder
1½ cups non-dairy creamer (I use 3 x 125 ml sachets Orley Whip™ Cook 'n Crème)
pinch salt and a little ground black pepper

FOR THE TOASTED WHOLE WHEAT CRUMBLES
1 health loaf (must be at least two days old)
1 tsp onion salt
½ tsp garlic salt
olive oil spray

Fry the chicken breasts and onions in a little oil in a soup pot until brown. Add the water and bring to the boil. Reduce the heat and simmer for 45 minutes.

Remove the chicken breasts from the soup and set the soup aside to cool slightly. (Keep the chicken breasts for toasted chicken mayonnaise or if you want a thicker texture, remove the skin and bones, cut up a breast or two and put it back into the soup.)

Drain all three tins of asparagus, reserving the liquid in a separate bowl. Combine this liquid with the cornflour, soup powder and non-dairy creamer and mix well.

Place two tins of the drained asparagus cuts into the cooled chicken soup and start blending it with a hand blender. Slowly pour in the cornflour mixture and continue blending.

Place the soup back onto the heat and bring to the boil, stirring it with a whisk as you do so. If the soup is too thick, add a little water and a pinch of salt. Once it starts boiling, gently fold in the last tin of asparagus, add black pepper and switch off the heat. Check for salt.

The last tin of asparagus added must not be blended, as you want the soup to have whole pieces. It's always better for people to see what soup they're eating without having to ask! When ready to serve, reheat the soup and serve with the bread crumbles.

WHOLE WHEAT CRUMBLES:
Cut off the first slice of bread. Hollow out the inside of the loaf by crumbling the bread with your fingers. These should have a chunkier texture than fine breadcrumbs. (Give the crusts to the birds!) Place the crumbles on a baking tray, sprinkle with the onion and garlic salt, and spray with olive oil spray. Bake uncovered at 140 °C for 1 hour.

SERVES 6

sawubona SAMPMEALIE SOUP

THERE ARE A FEW REASONS WHY THIS HAS TO BE MADE IN A LARGE SOUP POT, THE FIRST BEING THAT YOU CAN NEVER MAKE ENOUGH, THE SECOND THAT THE SAMP AND BEANS SWELL QUITE A BIT SO YOU'LL NEED TO KEEP ADDING WATER AND THE THIRD … WELL, I'LL THINK THAT UP AS WE GO ALONG!

½ cup small dried white beans

½ cup dried brown-speckled beans

½ cup barley

1 cup samp

1 piece of meaty shin *(Who's going to fight over the marrow?)*

1 piece of top rib

2 large sugar bones (oh yes, this is the third reason – the bones and soup meat also need space!)

3 chicken drumsticks

little oil for frying

3 large onions, chopped

4 cups grated carrot

3 Tbsp finely chopped flat-leaf parsley

4 litres water

3 beef stock cubes

5 medium potatoes, peeled and cubed (small)

salt and pepper

Rinse the beans, barley and samp well, place in a bowl, cover with 6 cups boiling water and leave to soak overnight. The following morning, discard the water and rinse the beans.

In a large soup pot fry the soup meat, bones and drumsticks in the oil. When lightly browned, remove from the pot and set aside.

Add a little more oil to the soup pot and fry the onions, carrots and flat-leaf parsley for about 10 minutes or until the onions start browning.

Put the soup meat, bones and drumsticks back in the soup pot and cover with the water. Scrape the bottom of the pot while adding the water as this is where all the lovely flavours are.

Crumble the beef stock cubes into the water. Add the potatoes, beans, barley and samp, and bring to the boil.

Reduce the heat, add salt and pepper to taste and simmer for about 4 hours.

Notes: You may find that you need to add more water. Although it is a thick soup, you'll have to judge this as it simmers. Some beans may be older and dryer than others and therefore need more water!

SERVES 10–12

wild Mexican
TOMATO SOUP

THIS IS A SIMPLE, NO-FUSS, 'SPICYISH' SOUP WITH A VARIETY OF INTERESTING TEXTURES. THE CONTRASTING SWEETNESS OF THE CORN AND THE VELVETY SMOOTHNESS OF THE GUACAMOLE SEEM TO SOOTHE THE PALATE. SERVE THIS WITH THE MEXICAN FIESTA (PAGE 94) AND YOU'LL HAVE EVERYBODY DOING THE *JARABE TAPATIO* MEXICAN HAT DANCE IN NO TIME!

4 large potatoes
4 cups boiling water
3 beef stock cubes, dissolved in
2 litres boiling water
1 x 200 g packet Spanish rice mix
1 x 410 g tin Mexican-style chopped tomatoes
1 x 410 g tin skinned and chopped tomatoes
1 cup tomato juice
2 Tbsp brown sugar
1 x 420 g tin baked beans
pinch salt and pepper to taste
1 x 420 g tin cream-style sweetcorn
fresh coriander to garnish

FOR THE GUACAMOLE TOPPING
3 Tbsp finely chopped fresh coriander
2 avocados, peeled and halved
½ tsp garlic salt

Peel and dice the potatoes (small cubes). Place them into a soup pot and cover with the boiling water. Bring to the boil and boil for about 15 minutes until soft, but not falling apart.

Add the beef stock and the rice without the spice mix (keep the spice mix for another Spanish dish!). Bring to the boil and leave to simmer, covered, for 40 minutes.

Meanwhile, blend the Mexican-style and skinned and chopped tomatoes with the tomato juice, brown sugar, baked beans, salt and pepper with a hand blender or in a food processor for a few seconds. It mustn't be too smooth as this should be a textured soup.

Add this blended mixture to the soup pot and leave to simmer on low for about 1 hour. Keep stirring every now and then to prevent the rice from sticking to the bottom of the pot.

Finally, add the cream-style sweetcorn and mix well. Bring to the boil, stirring as you do so, then switch off the heat and leave the soup to stand, covered, for about 30 minutes.

Prepare the guacamole topping. This can be done while making the soup and set aside in the fridge until needed.

GUACAMOLE TOPPING:
Blend together all the ingredients. While this is blending, slowly add ½ cup water, bit by bit (some avocados naturally have more water than others). This needs to be quite a soft, smooth topping that you can swirl with a tablespoon over the soup when serving.

When you're ready to serve, reheat the soup, drizzle the guacamole (room temperature) over the top and garnish with roughly chopped coriander.

SERVES 10–12

MUSHROOM SOUP

EVERY TIME I COOK WITH MUSHROOMS, I THINK OF A VERY SPECIAL MAN IN MY LIFE, MY LATE FATHER (OBM). WHENEVER WE ATE ANYTHING WITH MUSHROOMS, HE WOULD SAY, 'DON'T EAT TOO MANY MUSHROOMS OR YOU WON'T LEAVE 'MUSH ROOM' FOR ANYTHING ELSE!' AND THAT WOULD DEFINITELY BE THE CASE HERE AS THIS IS QUITE A HEARTY SOUP.

2 large onions, chopped
little oil for frying
500 g fresh mushrooms, sliced
3 chicken carcasses
3 litres water
1 x 200 g box Tastic™ Savoury Wild Rice
2 Tbsp mushroom soup powder
salt and pepper

Fry the onions in oil in a large soup pot. When glassy, add the mushrooms and fry until the water starts to evaporate.

Add the carcasses and 2 litres water. Allow to simmer, covered, for about 1½ hours.

Remove the carcasses from the pot, add the third litre of water, the wild rice with its spices, the mushroom soup mix, and salt and pepper to taste.

Leave to simmer, covered, for 1 hour on low heat.

Note: This is a really thick, hearty soup but if you feel it's too thick, add a little more water.

SERVES 6–8

'What are we … chopped liver?'

AWESOME
offal

Once upon a time … and it wasn't that long ago either, we had to grill and kosher liver at home. Today, thank goodness, we can order it from some butchers grilled and already koshered for us. I remember my mother having to kosher her own meat. I can still see those koshering racks, chunks of salt and lumps of 'something' floating about in aluminium buckets under our kitchen table. But come dinnertime, thank goodness, it had miraculously evolved into a magnificent roast.

Fortunately life took a dramatic turn in the '70s when a decision was made that all meat would be koshered on the butcher's premises. The backbreaking job of koshering meat at home was finally over and I've got the 'chutzpah' to complain about the occasional piece of liver!

Offal seemed such an awful name for wonderful delicacies such as pickled tongue, livers peri-peri and chopped liver. So I decided to change the word offal (or 'awful' as my children like to call it) to 'awesome'.

So, here are a few 'awesome' recipes that helped me to get my iron-deficient son to eat liver! It worked for me, I hope it does for you!

LIVER
and onions

FEELING SLUGGISH? THEN THERE'S NOTHING BETTER THAN A SHOT OF IRON! TWO OF THE BEST SOURCES OF IRON ARE LIVER AND RED MEAT. MAKE SURE YOU GET THE MAXIMUM BENEFIT BY DRINKING A GLASS OF ORANGE JUICE WITH IT AS THE VITAMIN C HELPS TO ABSORB THE IRON (IT HAS TO BE NEAT, OF COURSE, NO RUSSIAN ADDITIVES – I SAID IRON NOT IRON CURTAIN!)

500 g sliced and already grilled and koshered calf's/ox's liver
½ cup flour
3 large onions, cut in half and sliced into semicircles
little oil for frying
½ tsp freshly crushed garlic
¼ cup red wine (optional)
1 cup chicken stock (either home-made or 1 chicken stock cube dissolved in 1 cup hot water)
freshly ground black pepper (optional)

Wash the liver well to remove any traces of burnt bits. Cut the liver into the desired size and coat with the flour.

Fry the onions in oil until glassy, then add the garlic and toss for a minute or two. Add the liver to the onions and continue frying on medium heat until the onions are golden brown. Don't allow the pan to burn as this will give the gravy a bitter taste.

Add the wine, if using, and the chicken stock, stirring as you do so to get all the bits off the bottom of the pan. This, together with the onions, gives the gravy its delicious taste.

Leave the gravy to thicken and reduce slightly. If you feel your gravy is a little too thick, add a little more water and bring to the boil. Add salt and a little freshly ground black pepper and serve on a mound of mashed potato. Mmm, this so *geshmak*!

SERVES 4–5

quick and easy
CHICKEN LIVERS PERI-PERI

THANK GOODNESS WE DON'T HAVE TO KOSHER OUR OWN CHICKEN LIVERS TODAY! OTHERWISE, THE TITLE OF THIS RECIPE WOULD BE 'LONG, LABORIOUS LABOUR OF LOVE' AND NOT 'QUICK AND EASY'!

1 kg koshered chicken livers
(ready grilled)
2 large onions, chopped
1 heaped tsp freshly
crushed garlic
3 Tbsp peri-peri oil
½ cup red wine
1 Tbsp brown sugar
1 x 200 ml sachet
Ina Paarman's™ peri-peri sauce
1 Tbsp hot chilli sauce (optional)
2 Tbsp sweet chilli sauce
1 beef stock cube dissolved in
1 cup boiling water
1 chicken stock cube dissolved in
1 cup boiling water

Wash the chicken livers well to remove any bits of burnt edges, and separate the two halves to remove the middle vein.

Fry the onions and garlic in the peri-peri oil until lightly browned. Add the red wine and brown sugar, and bring to the boil.

Reduce the heat and leave the onions to simmer in the wine for about 5 minutes. Add the livers and increase the heat, stirring continuously so that the livers become well coated.

Add the peri-peri sauce, the hot and the sweet chilli sauces. Add the beef and chicken stocks and give it a good stir. Reduce the heat to low and simmer for at least 45 minutes, stirring every now and then.

Serve on a bed of rice.

SERVES 8–10

CHOPPED LIVER
and bagel

WHO SAYS CHOPPED LIVER HAS TO BE SERVED ONLY ON SHABBOS AND JEWISH HOLIDAYS? 'A CHOLESTEROL BOOST ON BAGEL', AS HE CALLS IT, IS MY BROTHER'S BEST FOR SUNDAY BREAKFAST!

4 large onions, chopped
1 tsp brown sugar
¼ cup oil/schmaltz for frying
(OK, so you'll start your diet on Monday!)
4 hard-boiled eggs
250 g ready-koshered chicken livers (ready grilled)
1 chicken stock cube dissolved in ½–¾ cup boiling water
salt and pepper

Fry the onions and sugar in the oil or schmaltz in a large pot until golden brown. (Caramelising the onions is the secret to that special tasting liver!)

While the onions are frying, hard boil the eggs. Remove the onions from the heat once they are brown.

Wash the chicken livers in cold water and remove any burnt bits, membranes and sinews. Add the livers to the onions and mix well until all the livers are well coated with onions and oil. Add half to three-quarters of the dissolved chicken stock, reserving a bit in case you want to add it once you have minced everything together.

Place it back onto the stove, bring to the boil, mixing well and scraping all the brown bits off the bottom of the pot. That's where the flavour sits! Once it starts to boil, remove from the heat.

Mince the liver, onions and eggs with a hand or electric mincer. Add salt and pepper to taste.

Should you want a smoother texture (only you can be the judge of that – you know your family!), add the reserved chicken stock.

Notes: A few ways to serve chopped liver.
- Place a bowl of chopped liver on a large plate. Place a spreading knife alongside it and surround the bowl of liver with bagel chips (available at most kosher bakeries and supermarkets).
- To make liver pâté, mince the already-minced liver through the machine again and add a little chicken stock, which will give it an even smoother texture. If you want to make a really smooth liver pâté, place all the ingredients before mincing straight from the frying pan into a food processor and blend until smooth.
- Decorate the liver as you would for a special occasion with grated boiled egg in any creative design.

SERVES 6–8

AWESOME OFFAL

GLAZED PICKLED TONGUE
and parsley butter bean sauce

A TONGUE TWISTER TO TRULY TANTALISE YOUR TASTE BUDS!

1 pickled tongue
6 bay leaves
1 Tbsp peppercorns
1 onion
1 carrot
2 sticks celery
1 Tbsp coarse salt

FOR THE GLAZE
1 heaped tsp mustard powder
½ cup stock (water tongue was boiling in)
1 Tbsp ginger syrup
1 Tbsp apricot jam

FOR THE PARSLEY BUTTER BEAN SAUCE
1 onion, chopped
little oil for frying
1 tsp crushed garlic
1 bunch Italian parsley, finely chopped
1 x 410 g tin butter beans
1 heaped Tbsp cornflour
½ cup non-dairy creamer (either Rich's™ or Orley Whip™)
1 cup water
salt

Place all the ingredients into a pot and cover with water. Boil, covered, for approximately 2 hours until the tongue is soft.

Retain ½ cup strained stock for the glaze and discard the rest of the liquid.

Remove the tongue from the pot and when cool, peel off the outside layer.

GLAZE:

Preheat the oven to 200–220 °C 30 minutes before serving.

Combine all the glaze ingredients, mix well and cover the entire tongue with the glaze. Place the tongue on a large piece of aluminium foil. Bring the foil up on the sides to join in the middle so that it lies loosely around the tongue, ballooning it.

Place it in an ovenproof dish and bake for about 15 minutes. Open the foil parcel (be careful of the hot steam!), baste the tongue well with its own juices and continue to bake, uncovered, for another 5–10 minutes.

Serve immediately with the parsley butter bean sauce. The sauce can be made a day ahead and reheated on the stove or in the microwave.

PARSLEY BUTTER BEAN SAUCE:

Fry the onion in a little oil until limp. Keep stirring as you add the garlic and parsley. Remove from the heat and set aside.

Drain the butter beans and reserve the liquid. In a bowl, combine the cornflour, butter bean liquid, creamer and water, and mix well. Pour the mixture over the onion and mix well.

Return this mixture to the heat and stir until it thickens, then add the beans and continue stirring until the bean mixture starts to bubble.

Remove from the heat, add salt to taste and reheat before serving.

SERVES 4–5

'Oy vey! here comes a tall order ...'

MAINS

Beef

PRIME RIB
with roasted garlic and horseradish crust

THERE'S NO DOUBT AS TO WHY THIS CUT OF MEAT HAS THIS NAME – IT CERTAINLY IS THE PRIME CHOICE FOR A SPECIAL OCCASION. IT DRAWS ITS NATURAL FLAVOUR FROM THE BONES AND THEREFORE NEEDS VERY LITTLE 'PATZKKERING' OR PAMPERING. A LIGHT GARLIC AND HORSERADISH CRUST ON THE OUTSIDE IS ENOUGH TO GIVE IT ALL THE FLAVOUR IT NEEDS.

1 x 3 kg prime rib roast on the bone

FOR THE CRUST
1 head garlic
1 Tbsp horseradish (ready made or see page 43)
1 Tbsp brown sugar
2 tsp coarsely ground black pepper
1 Tbsp prepared grainy mustard
½ cup olive oil
2 Tbsp breadcrumbs

Preheat the oven to 170 °C. Wash the roast well but don't remove too much fat off the flap as this keeps it moist while roasting. Place it into the oven on the bottom rack, uncovered and unspiced, for 80 minutes. Make sure that the roast stands on its flat-boned base with the ribs upwards. Remove it from the oven and set it aside to cool.

CRUST:
While the meat is roasting, pop the head of garlic into the oven for about 20 minutes or until its outer leaves are brown. Remove it from the oven and press the cloves out of their skin into a bowl. The flesh should be quite soft and squeeze out easily.

Mash the garlic, then add the horseradish, sugar, black pepper, mustard, oil and breadcrumbs, and mix well. Should you wish to remove any excess fat from the roast, now would be a good time.

With the palm of your hand pat the crust mixture onto the cooled roast so that the entire outside is well coated.

Place the roast back into the oven and continue roasting, uncovered, at 180 °C for a further 1 hour until the crust is nicely browned. Should you prefer your meat a little more well done, leave it in for a further 20–30 minutes.

Remove the meat from the oven and allow it to rest on a carving board for a few minutes. While it's resting, add 2 cups cold water mixed with 2 Tbsp gravy powder and 1 Tbsp flour to the juices at the bottom of the roasting pan, bring to the boil, strain and there you have a delicious gravy!

SERVES 8–10

42

'CHRAIN'
minced horseradish sauce

MY EYES START WATERING AT THE VERY THOUGHT OF MAKING 'CHRAIN' (HORSERADISH). FROM THE MOMENT I START PEELING THE HORSERADISH THE TRANSFORMATION INTO A BLACK-EYED MONSTER BEGINS. AS THE TEARS WASH THE MASCARA DOWN MY FACE I KEEP REMINDING MYSELF THAT THE BURNT NASAL PASSAGES AND TEMPORARY LOSS OF EYESIGHT ARE SHORT LIVED! THE ANTICIPATION OF HEARING THE FAMILY SAY, 'THIS IS YOUR BEST VINTAGE EVER!' PUSHES ME THROUGH THAT PAIN BARRIER. SO, DON'T LET ME BE THE ONLY HORSERADISH HEROINE AROUND, JOIN ME ON THE 'CHRAIN TRAIN'. IT WILL BE WORTH THE TRIP.

750 g–1 kg horseradish (if you're going to make chrain, make it worthwhile – make it big!)
2 cups white vinegar
1 cup water
½ cup white sugar
1 Tbsp salt

Peel or scrub the horseradish with steel wool, cut it into 1 cm slices and mince in a mincer (fine blade) or blend in a food processor.

If using a processor, add a cup of vinegar to the horseradish before you blend it otherwise the blades could stick!

Place the minced horseradish in a large plastic bowl, add the rest of the ingredients and mix well.

At this point you will have to call in the experts to taste for salt or extra sugar, but be careful because they'll all give you different opinions!

When the taste is just right, place the chrain into sterilised glass jars and add a little vinegar to cover the horseradish to prevent it from drying out. Seal the jars with fresh seals. Now you can wash your face and wait another six months before making chrain again!

MAKES ENOUGH TO LAST FOR ABOUT 6 MONTHS

Rolls Royce
RIB ROAST

SCOTCH FILLET IS A VERY ELEGANT CUT OF BEEF. IT MAKES A STATEMENT IN A SIMPLE, YET EFFECTIVE WAY AND THAT'S EXACTLY HOW IT SHOULD BE COOKED. IT REALLY IS A CASE OF LESS IS BEST WITH THIS ROAST.

3 kg Scotch fillet roast

FOR THE HERBED OIL
1½ cups olive oil
¼ cup lemon juice
8 sage leaves
6 sprigs rosemary
½ tsp salt
2 tsp coarsely ground pepper
2 tsp crushed garlic
1 Tbsp mustard seeds or
1 tsp brown grainy mustard

HERBED OIL:

Place all the ingredients in a bottle or jar with a tight-fitting lid and give it a good shake up. This should keep for at least 3 weeks.

Preheat the oven to 220 °C. Place the roast in a roasting pan. Paint the entire roast with the herbed oil, then place in the oven, covered, for 1 hour. Reduce the heat to 180 °C, and roast, uncovered, for a further 30 minutes. Turn the roast over and roast, uncovered, for another 20 minutes.

Oven temperatures do vary, so rather undercook than overcook the meat. It can always go back into the oven if you prefer it well done.

SERVES 10–12

THE 10 CARVING TIPS

1. It's far easier to carve a roast off the bone than on the bone.
2. Choose a carving board with a deep groove around the edge to collect the juices.
3. Select a carving knife that is comfortable to hold.
4. It will be worth your while paying a little extra and getting a good knife with a blade that will sharpen well and cut to perfection.
5. It's essential that a carving knife be kept sharp at all times, therefore a good sharpener is just as important as the carver.
6. Slicing meat too soon after it comes out of the oven can cause the juices to run out too quickly. Rather allow the meat to rest a little by 'tenting' some tin foil around it to keep the heat in.
7. Always sharpen then wash and dry a knife before using it.
8. Always cut against the run of the grain.
9. Always place the knife beneath a piece of already sliced meat, steadying it from above with a fork, and transfer it onto a plate.
10. The more muscular roasts should be carved into very thin slices, whereas with more tender roasts this is not necessary.

'rub me up the right way'
ROAST

I HAVE USED A FRENCH-TRIMMED PRIME RIB ROAST IN THIS RECIPE. IT REALLY IS A VERY NEAT, ELEGANT ROAST AND CERTAINLY IS THE PRIME CHOICE FOR A SPECIAL OCCASION. SO WHEN THE IN-LAWS COME FOR DINNER THEY'LL EITHER SAY, 'WOW, SHE KNOWS HOW TO COOK', OR 'WOW, SHE KNOWS HOW TO SPEND HIS MONEY!' WHATEVER THE COST, IT WILL BE WELL WORTH IT!

3 kg French-trimmed rib roast
oil for rubbing

FOR THE RUB
1 tsp dried sage
1 tsp dried thyme
1 Tbsp mustard seeds or
1 tsp mustard powder
½ tsp garlic powder
½ tsp onion powder
1 Tbsp brown sugar
1½ tsp paprika
1 tsp ground black pepper
¼ tsp ground cumin
pinch chilli powder
½ tsp ground ginger

RUB:

These spices make a wonderful rub, which can be used for almost any roast. Combine the spices and mix well. With the palm of your hand rub some oil over the roast and then rub the spice mixture over it, making sure you get into all the crevices.

Preheat the oven to 180 °C. Once you have covered the entire roast with oil and spices, cover it with aluminium foil and roast it in the oven for 45–60 minutes.

Remove the foil and continue cooking, uncovered, for a further 45–60 minutes. Baste the roast every so often with its own juices. This cooking time should be enough for a rare roast. However, should you wish it to be medium to well done it will need another 30–45 minutes.

Notes: You could also use a prime rib roast on the bone, which is the same cut but hasn't had all the meat trimmed off the bone. This is a great roast for those who like tucking into meaty bones!

Providing roasting times is quite a difficult task as it depends on many things, e.g. the size of your oven (larger ovens take longer) and whether the meat is taken from the fridge or is at room temperature. In an ideal world it would be wonderful to give exact roasting times, but each person must get to know his/her own oven.

SERVES 8–10

SHOULDER ROAST
in peppercorn jacket with Yorkshire pudding

SHOULDER BOLO IS A VERY LEAN, BONELESS, SOLID PIECE OF MEAT. IT IS USED IN MOST DELICATESSENS AS THEIR RARE ROAST BEEF CUT AND, BECAUSE IT IS VERY THINLY SLICED, THEY CAN GET AWAY WITH DRY ROASTING IT RATHER THAN HAVING TO BRAISE OR STEW IT. SO WE'RE GOING TO FOLLOW SUIT, AND ALTHOUGH MOST OF US DON'T HAVE THOSE WONDERFUL, AUTOMATIC MEAT SLICERS, THERE'S NOTHING A LITTLE CONCENTRATION AND A SHARP CARVING KNIFE CAN'T DO. JUST REMEMBER TO 'KEEP IT THIN'.

1 heaped Tbsp prepared whole grain mustard
½ tsp dried tarragon
½ tsp dried thyme
1 level tsp paprika
½ tsp garlic salt
1 Tbsp brown sugar
3 Tbsp oil
2 tsp crushed, tri-coloured peppercorns
2–2.5 kg shoulder bolo
oil for roasting
2 large onions, sliced into rings

FOR THE YORKSHIRE PUDDING
4 large eggs
2 cups water
1½ cups self-raising flour, sifted
1 tsp salt

Preheat the oven to 220 °C. Combine the mustard, tarragon, thyme, paprika, garlic salt, sugar, oil and peppercorns.

With the palm of your hand cover the entire roast evenly with this mixture. Pour a little oil in a roasting pan and add half the onion rings. Place the bolo on top of the onions and cover the top of the roast with the rest of the onions.

Roast in the oven, covered, for 40 minutes. Reduce the heat to 180 °C and continue cooking, uncovered, for 15 minutes. Turn the meat over and roast for a further 15 minutes.

Remove the roast from the oven at this point. It will not be ready yet (unless you like it very rare) and will still need an extra 30 minutes, but to co-ordinate it with the Yorkshire pudding, which takes about 25–30 minutes, I prefer to take it out now and leave it to stand while making up the Yorkshire pudding. While the roast is taking a 'breather', you will notice that it gives off the most wonderful, tasty juices, which will be used later in the gravy.

YORKSHIRE PUDDING:
Preheat the oven to 220 °C.

This pudding can either be made in a muffin tin and served as individual puddings, or in a large, shallow roasting pan.

Place a tablespoon of oil in each muffin cup or, if using a roasting pan, enough oil to line the bottom (about 1 cm deep).

Blend the eggs and water in a food processor, or in a liquidiser like my mother does! Add the flour and salt, and continue beating or blending.

Place the oiled muffin or roasting pan into the oven and heat the oil for about 5–10 minutes.

CONTINUED ON PAGE 50

Remove the pan from the oven but be careful, as it will be very hot! Close the oven door to keep in the heat.

Use a jug to pour the batter into the individual muffin cups or roasting pan. It should come halfway up the sides.

Just before putting the meat back into the oven with the Yorkshire pudding, drain the juices at the bottom of the roasting pan into a small saucepan, which will be used to make up the gravy. Get the meat ready to be placed back into the oven for its final heat up. If you think the meat is not brown enough, put it back into the oven, uncovered. If it is brown enough, cover it with aluminium foil.

Reduce the oven temperature to 180 °C and place the pudding into the oven with the meat for 25 minutes or until the pudding puffs up and becomes golden brown in colour.

Do not open the oven, as the pudding will deflate! So remember, you can't touch the meat either!

Make sure all your other vegetable dishes are ready so that you can serve the meat and pudding as they come out of the oven.

DARK BROWN GRAVY:

While the meat is heating through and roasting a little longer with the Yorkshire pudding, make up the gravy by combining 2 Tbsp gravy powder, 1 heaped Tbsp flour and 1½ cups cold water. Mix well to form a lump-free consistency and add to the meat juices from the roasting pan.

Bring the gravy to the boil, stirring with a whisk as you do so. Reduce the heat and allow to simmer for a few minutes. Reheat when ready to serve.

SERVES 8–10

CHUCKLEBERRY
spin

THIS GOT ITS NAME QUITE SIMPLY BECAUSE I WAS IN A FLAT SPIN ONE NIGHT HAVING FORGOTTEN I'D INVITED PEOPLE OVER AND IT WAS JUST AFTER YOMTOV, SO THERE WAS NO MEAT! WELL, I FOUND A PIECE OF FROZEN CHUCK ON THE BONE AND HAD A GOOD CHUCKLE WHEN THE VISITORS EXCLAIMED, 'YOU SEE, THE BUTCHER'S WIFE KNOWS WHICH CUTS TO PICK!' IF ONLY THEY KNEW HOW, WITH EACH SLICE, I PRAYED THAT IT HAD COOKED THROUGH!

4 onions, sliced into rings

5 sprigs fresh thyme or 1 tsp dried thyme to mix into the rub

½ cup olive oil + ¼ cup for meat rub

2 kg chuck on the bone (defrosted, if you have time!)

1 tsp crushed garlic

1 heaped Tbsp freshly grated ginger

1 heaped tsp paprika

1 Tbsp mustard powder

¼ cup soy sauce

4 large potatoes, peeled and cut into quarters

Place the sliced onions (I think this is the secret ingredient) and the sprigs of thyme at the bottom of a large roasting pan.

Pour ½ cup oil over the onions and thyme and place the roast on top of this. Mix all the other ingredients (except the potatoes) in a small glass bowl (if you don't have fresh thyme add the 1 tsp dried thyme) and with the palm of your hand rub this mixture into the meat into every little nook and cranny. Place the potatoes into the roasting pan with the meat.

Roast, uncovered, for 40 minutes at 200 °C, then reduce the heat to 170 °C and roast, covered, for a further 1½ hours. Keep basting the roast.

If you feel the roast is not brown enough, remove the lid after 1 hour and roast, uncovered, for the last 30 minutes until brown. If you prefer your meat well done, place the cover back onto the roast, reduce the heat to 160 °C and roast for a further 25–35 minutes.

SERVES 6–8

bronzed BAG OF BEEF

THIS HEALTHY LOOKING MEAL IN A BAG IS ONE OF THOSE TASTY, LOYAL, NEVER-LET-YOU-DOWN KIND OF RECIPES. ALTHOUGH THE MEAT AND VEGETABLES ARE IN A BAG, THE BAG DOESN'T ACT AS A 'SUNBLOCK'. THE TRANSPARENCY OF IT ALLOWS THE MEAT AND VEGETABLES TO 'TAN' TO A PERFECT SHADE OF DARK BROWN. THEY SAY THERE'S NOTHING QUITE LIKE A BRONZE-TANNED PIECE OF OILED BEEF!

4 parsnips, cut into 5 cm chunks
8 baby beetroot
2 red onions, cut into quarters
250 g baby onions
1 head garlic
3 sprigs thyme
½–¾ cup oil
1 Tbsp brown sugar
coarse salt
1 large cooking bag
2 kg roll of beef, spiced

Place all the vegetables with the thyme in a bowl and coat with the oil. Sprinkle with the sugar and coarse salt. Place the vegetables into a large cooking bag together with the meat. Roast for 2 hours at 180 °C. Don't turn or touch the meat as it may squash the vegetables. Serve with rice and peas.

Notes: Ask your butcher to spice the roll of beef with barbecue spices.
   Carrots, cubed butternut and baby potatoes can also be added.

SERVES 8

wrapped BEEF

MY BROTHER BOUGHT A NEW WEBER™ BRAAI/BARBECUE AND FOR TWO WEEKS SOLID WE TESTED EVERYTHING FROM T-BONES TO TURKEY. BUT THIS WAS THE ONE THAT GOT THE HIGH FIVE!

2 kg roll of beef or Scotch fillet
2 cups basting sauce (see Butcher's Baster page 16 or your favourite ready-made)
3 sheets brown paper (ask your butcher to include it with the parcel)
1 x 450 ml can beer

Marinate the beef in the basting sauce overnight. The following day wrap the beef (together with all the basting sauce) in brown paper, folding in the sides and rolling it up one sheet at a time. Place the parcel into a roasting dish, and pour the can of beer over it. Turn it over a few times so that the paper absorbs the beer. The moisture helps to prevent the paper from burning too quickly.

Light the coals and after 45–60 minutes place the roast onto the grid and cover with the dome. The air vent in the dome should be slightly open. Don't worry about the paper burning; by the time the paper has burnt down to the last layer, the roast will almost be ready!

After 30 minutes turn the roast over, leave the dome off for 5 minutes then cover it again for a further 30 minutes.

Remove the dome. You will notice the paper peeling away from the roast. Cut the paper lengthwise off the roast and remove it completely. Try to retain some of the juices on the bottom of the paper and pour this over the top of the meat.

Allow the roast to get a little more crispy and brown, uncovered (dome off), on the grid. It should only take 10–15 minutes per side for rare to medium meat. Leave it a little longer if you want it well done. Serve immediately.

Tip: When making a braai or barbecue fire, mound your briquettes like a pyramid and when the coals are glowing, disperse them into a single layer.

SERVES 8

RAISON D'ÊTRE RAISIN-RIB
'the reliable roast'

I'VE ALWAYS CALLED RAISIN-RIB THE 'RELIABLE ROAST'. IT'S A SOFT, TASTY PIECE OF MEAT THAT NEEDS VERY LITTLE PAMPERING AND IF YOU FORGET TO PUT ON ITS MASCARA OR ADD TOO MUCH LIPSTICK, IT STILL COMES OUT LOOKING GOOD. IT DOES, HOWEVER, ENJOY A LONG, HOT SOAK IN THE BATH!

2–2.5 kg raisin-rib roast
3 Tbsp peri-peri or sunflower oil
2 large onions, cut in half and sliced into rings
1 tsp coffee powder, dissolved in ¾ cup boiling water
2 heaped Tbsp brown sugar
½ cup tomato sauce
½ cup tomato jam (this gives the meat a nice glaze)
2 Tbsp soy sauce
½ cup hot chutney
1 Tbsp grainy prepared mustard
salt and pepper

Preheat the oven to 180 °C. Place the roast into an ovenproof dish or roasting pan.

Pour a little oil into a saucepan and fry the onions until golden brown. Add the rest of the ingredients, bring to the boil, stirring continuously, then reduce the heat and allow it to simmer for a few minutes.

Pour over the meat and roast in the oven, uncovered, for 30 minutes. Turn the roast over and roast it, again uncovered, for a further 30 minutes.

Reduce the heat to 160 °C and let it enjoy its long, hot relaxation period, covered, in the oven for about 1–1½ hours.

Remove the lid and baste the roast. It should have a nice rich, dark glaze to it. If you find it hasn't, turn up the heat a little to about 200 °C and cook it a little longer until it gets that thick, glazed, saucy look!

SERVES 8–10

thyme out
ROUND BOLO ROAST

THIS IS A LOVELY ROAST FOR FOUR. IT'S A SMALL, WHOLE PIECE WEIGHING ABOUT 1 KG. IT IS AN EXTREMELY LEAN ROAST AND FOR THIS REASON I USE A COMBINATION OF OIL AND HERBS TO KEEP IT MOIST AND BROWN. THERE IS NOTHING NICER THAN FRESH HERBS; HOWEVER, DRIED HERBS ALSO WORK WELL IN THIS RECIPE.

1 large onion, sliced into rings
6–8 sprigs thyme or 1 tsp dried thyme
½ cup oil
½ tsp crushed garlic
½ tsp paprika
½ tsp ground black pepper
pinch ground ginger
1 heaped tsp prepared grainy mustard
1 heaped tsp brown onion soup powder
1 round bolo roast (vacuum-packed and left in the fridge for one week – then either use or freeze)

Preheat the oven to 200 °C. Place the sliced onion rings on the base of a small roasting pan or ovenproof dish. Place the thyme sprigs on top of the onion rings (if you are using dried thyme, sprinkle it over the onions) and set the roasting pan aside.

Mix the oil, garlic, paprika, black pepper, ginger, prepared mustard and onion soup powder until well combined. Rub this over the meat making sure that it is really well coated. Reserve ±2 tablespoons of the oil mixture to brush on before serving.

Heat a frying pan until very hot and sear the roast on all sides (a minute or two on each side). Remove from the pan and place into the roasting dish with the onions and thyme. Bake, uncovered, for 25 minutes.

Turn the meat over, baste it and continue cooking on the other side for a further 20 minutes. Turn it over again and brush with the reserved oil mixture. Crisp it up for a few minutes so that it gets a nice golden brown look!

Tip: As the cooking time for a small roast is a lot shorter than for a large roast, it doesn't really have enough time to get that dark, crispy, roasted look on the outside that a larger roast would get. A larger roast has a longer roasting time, which allows the outside of the meat to brown and the fat to become crisp before the centre of the roast becomes overcooked. So, when making a small roast weighing about 1 kg, brown it in a very hot pan, searing it on all sides first before putting it in the roasting pan in a preheated oven. This helps to prevent overcooking, and it still has that lovely dark, roasted look. A roast just under 1 kg (like a round bolo) cooked this way would only need about 45–55 minutes in a hot oven (200 °C).

SERVES 3–4

MINI BEEF WELLINGTONS
wrapped in mushroom stuffing with sage-infused gravy

I ATTEMPTED TO MAKE A NOUVELLE CUISINE DINNER ONE EVENING, PAINSTAKINGLY CUTTING OUT FLORAL DESIGNS FROM VEGETABLES AND DELICATELY HAND PAINTING EACH PLATE WITH GRAVY. I CONFIDENTLY PLACED THE MEAL IN FRONT OF THE CRITICS – OOPS, I MEAN FAMILY. THE COMMENTS WENT SOMETHING LIKE THIS, 'MOM, HAVE YOU GIVEN UP ON THE COOKING AND STARTED ART CLASSES?'; 'DO WE GET A LOAF OF BREAD AND PEANUT BUTTER AFTER THIS MEAL?'; 'THESE ARE SAMPLES, RIGHT, SUPPER'S STILL TO FOLLOW?'. NO, THAT WAS IT, BUT SOMETHING INSIDE HAD WARNED ME TO MAKE EXTRA!

1.5 kg cubed Scotch fillet (ask your butcher to cut them into 3 cm cubes)
1 cup Italian salad dressing
¾ cup flour mixed with 1 Tbsp gravy powder
oil for frying
1 Tbsp flour and 1 Tbsp gravy powder dissolved in 2 cups water (for gravy)
6–8 sage leaves
1 x 100 g box poultry stuffing mix
1 x 450 g tin mushroom pieces
1 x 500 g box phyllo pastry
salt to taste

Marinate the cubed beef overnight (or 6–8 hours) in the salad dressing. Once marinated, remove the beef from the dressing and discard the dressing. Dip each cube of beef into the flour and gravy mixture ensuring that all the pieces are well coated.

Fry the meat (a few pieces at a time) in a large frying pan until they are evenly browned. They still have to go into the oven to cook a little more on the inside. Once all the meat has been fried, reduce the heat and add the flour and gravy mixture to the pan, stirring well and ensuring that you lift all the brown bits off the bottom. Remove from the heat, add the sage and allow it to infuse the liquid.

Make up the stuffing mixture as per the instructions on the packet, then add the drained mushrooms and allow to cool.

Preheat the oven to 160 °C. Take one full sheet of phyllo pastry and fold it in half, then in half again to one-quarter of its size. Place 1 tablespoon of stuffing into the centre of the pastry, smooth it out a bit and place one piece of meat on top of it. Draw the phyllo up around the sides of the meat, twist it in the middle and place it into a lightly greased muffin tin. Continue in this way until you've used all the meat. Spray with olive oil and bake for 20–25 minutes until golden brown. Use the gravy to garnish.

Note: It's difficult to say how many to serve per person. My sons are growing boys with healthy appetites 'keyn Aynhoreh' (no curse should come to them and they should continue to eat well!) and three each just didn't do it for them!

SERVES 6

MAINS – BEEF

RYAN'S SHINY GLAZED BEEF SPARE RIBS
and mambo mango salsa

THAT FAMOUS NURSERY RHYME ABOUT JACK SPRAT NOT BEING ABLE TO EAT ANY FAT COULD HAVE BEEN WRITTEN FOR MY SON RYAN! IF THERE IS A SLIGHT HINT OF FAT ON HIS MEAT, HE WON'T EAT IT. BEEF RIBS ARE HIS FAVOURITE – YES, THESE ARE THOSE LOVELY, SHINY GLAZED RIBS THAT HAVE THAT BITE-INTO-ME LOOK!

3 racks plain beef steakhouse ribs OR 3 racks smoked beef steakhouse ribs
(1 rack usually feeds 2–3 people)

FOR THE GLAZE
3 Tbsp soy sauce
3 Tbsp chutney
3 Tbsp apricot jam
3 Tbsp tomato jam
1 Tbsp honey
1 tsp crushed garlic
2 Tbsp brown sugar
2 Tbsp fresh lemon juice
1 Tbsp ginger syrup
1 tsp hot peri-peri sauce

FOR THE MAMBO MANGO SALSA
1 ripe mango, chopped
1 orange/yellow and 1 red pepper, seeded and chopped
1 tomato, seeded and chopped
1 avocado, roughly chopped
2 heaped Tbsp finely chopped fresh coriander
1 small onion, finely chopped
1 red hot chilli (optional)
2 tsp honey
juice of 1 lime or ½ lemon
salt and pepper

GLAZE:
Combine all the ingredients for the glaze (reserving a little in a separate bowl for the final basting). Preheat the oven to 180 °C. Paint the ribs with the glaze ensuring that each rib is well coated.

Bake in the oven, uncovered, for 45 minutes (25 minutes if the ribs are smoked) with the meaty side down and the back of the bones facing you. Turn the ribs over so that the meaty side faces you, and bake for a further 25–30 minutes (20 minutes if the ribs are smoked) or until a dark honey brown colour.

Give the ribs a final basting with the reserved glaze and bake for another 10–15 minutes. If you feel they are not dark or crispy enough, turn the oven up to 220 °C but keep basting them every few minutes as they will go dark quite quickly on higher heat.

MAMBO MANGO SALSA:
This salsa (Spanish for sauce) is a delicious light accompaniment to almost any meat and is a rhythmic combination of cold fresh herbs, fruits and vegetables, the only 'hot arrangement' here being the optional chilli!

Combine all the ingredients. Adjust to your taste and refrigerate.

A nice idea when serving this is to slice a large onion into thicker than normal rings from the thickest part of the onion. Place an onion ring on each plate and put salsa into each ring, the ring forming a border around the salsa.

Notes: Please note that cooking times are different for plain ribs and smoked ribs, as the smoked ribs are already cooked! I prefer to cut the ribs individually, as this makes them crispy all over when baked.

SERVES 6

TOP-RIB ROAST
to top 'em all

ONE OF MY FAVOURITE MEAT DISHES IS A TOP-RIB ROAST. IT IS SUCH AN UNCOMPLICATED, FORGIVING ROAST. NO MATTER WHAT YOU DO TO IT OR HOW MANY TESTS YOU PUT IT THROUGH, IT BEARS NO 'FARRIBLES' (GRUDGES) AND JUST KEEPS COMING OUT ON TOP! THE MEAT IS CLOSE TO THE BONE, MAKING IT A VERY TASTY ROAST. IT SATISFIES THOSE WHO LOVE TO 'MUNCH ON BONES' AND THOSE WHO PREFER ELEGANTLY SLICED LEAN PIECES OF BEEF. I TOLD YOU IT WAS A PEOPLE PLEASER!

2–2.5 kg top-rib roast

FOR THE GLAZE
¼ **cup orange marmalade**
4 **cloves garlic, crushed**
2 **Tbsp soy sauce**
¼ **cup brown sugar**
¼ **cup oil**
½ **tsp very hot chilli sauce**
1 **Tbsp prepared Hot English mustard**

GLAZE:

Heat all the ingredients for the glaze on the stove or in the microwave. When cool, rub the glaze all over the roast, ensuring that it is well covered.

Preheat the oven to 200 °C. Place the meat into a roasting pan, bone side down with the meat facing upwards, and roast it, covered, for 1 hour.

Reduce the heat to 180 °C, turn the roast over and roast, uncovered, for a further 30 minutes, basting every now and then.

After 30 minutes turn the roast over again with the meaty side facing upwards and allow it to brown for a further 25–30 minutes.

Slice against the grain and serve either on or off the bone. Most people prefer it on the bone.

SERVES 5–6

smoked
TOP-RIB ROAST

THIS WAS AN EXPERIMENT TO SATISFY ALL – THOSE WHO LOVE BONES AND THOSE WHO LOVE MEAT. BUT EVEN BETTER THAN THAT IS THAT IT SMELLS SO GOOD WHEN COOKING THAT THE VEGETARIANS START THINKING TWICE! AS THIS CUT OF MEAT HAS TO BE PICKLED AND SMOKED BY YOUR BUTCHER, IT'S BEST TO GIVE HIM AT LEAST TWO DAYS' NOTICE.

**1 smoked top-rib roast
(this normally feeds
3–4 hungry people)
1 cup mild or hot chutney
(whichever you prefer)
2 Tbsp tomato jam
2 Tbsp apricot jam
1 heaped tsp prepared mustard**

Preheat the oven to 180 °C. Wash the meat in cold water.

Don't be in a hurry to cut too much fat off the roast as this keeps it moist while roasting and most of the fat will burn off while cooking. However, if you feel there is an excess, trim it.

Combine the chutney, jams and mustard, mix well and cover the entire roast with the mixture. Roast, uncovered, for 45–60 minutes.

If you find that it gets too dark too quickly, cover it with aluminium foil. This can be removed towards the end to crisp it up. It really needs to cook for a minimum of 45–60 minutes so that it heats right through the roast. When purchasing this roast from your butcher, it is already cooked. All you need to do is crisp it up a little and allow it to turn a dark caramel brown.

This is delicious served with mashed onion potatoes (see page 175) and the mustard sauce from the glazed corn beef recipe (page 66).

SERVES 4

twisted BRISKET

IF THERE IS ONE THING MY BROTHER-IN-LAW HATES, IT'S FRUIT WITH MEAT. TO HIM FRUIT BELONGS IN A FRUIT SALAD AND NOT IN A MEAT DISH. HOWEVER, TO THIS DAY WE CALL IT BRISKET WITH A TWIST OR 'TWISTED BRISKET' AND HE'S NEVER WORKED OUT WHAT THE TWIST IS!

1 Tbsp cornflour
2.5 kg fresh brisket
little oil for frying
1 beef stock cube dissolved in
1 cup boiling water
1 x 410 g tin apricot halves in juice
2 Tbsp apricot jam
½ cup soy sauce
1 Tbsp lemon juice
1 Tbsp peri-peri sauce
½ cup hot chutney
4 cloves garlic
1 tsp grated fresh ginger
1 Tbsp tomato paste
3 Tbsp onion soup powder
1 tsp curry powder

Preheat the oven to 160 °C. Rub the cornflour over the entire roast and fry it in a little hot oil on top of the stove, just to seal it. Remove from the pan and place in a roasting dish. Add the beef stock to the pan and bring to the boil, scraping up the bits at the bottom of the pan. Remove from the heat and set aside.

Combine all the remaining ingredients in a bowl, add the beef stock and blend until smooth. Pour over the meat and cover with a lid or aluminium foil.

Roast in the oven for 2 hours.

Remove the covering, turn the heat up to 180 °C and roast for another 1–1½ hours, basting every so often until the sauce thickens and darkens.

SERVES 8–10

hot tray
JAM AND CHILLI BRISKET

IT WAS VERY LATE ONE EVENING AND WITH 'EYES WIDE SHUT' I WATCHED MY SISTER-IN-LAW IN DALLAS PREPARE A MEAL FOR THE FOLLOWING NIGHT'S DINNER! ALL SHE WOULD HAVE TO DO IS 'STICK IT ON THE HOT TRAY THE FOLLOWING MORNING AND BY THAT EVENING WE'D HAVE A WONDERFUL MEAL!' IT WAS AS SIMPLE AS THAT, AND THAT'S EXACTLY WHAT HAPPENED!

½ cup flour
2 Tbsp gravy powder
2–2.5 kg fresh brisket

FOR THE SAUCE
3 Tbsp grape jam
¼ cup red wine
(regular Shabbat wine is fine)
½ cup hot chutney
1 Tbsp hot chilli sauce
2 Tbsp sweet chilli sauce
¼ cup soy sauce
1 tsp crushed garlic
1 tsp grated fresh ginger

Combine the flour and gravy powder in a bowl and rub over the entire piece of beef.

Sear the outside of the meat in a hot, lightly oiled, heavy-base pan until dark brown. This should take 8–10 minutes if the pan is really hot. (I use a large cast-iron pot but my sister-in-law used a large frying pan then transferred it to a thick disposable aluminium roasting pan.) Make sure all the sides of the brisket come into contact with the pan to get it evenly browned. Remove from the heat, place in a roasting dish and add the following sauce.

SAUCE:

Combine all the ingredients and pour over the meat. Cover with a lid or aluminium foil and place in the fridge until the following morning.

The next day, place the meat onto a hot tray, switch it on and leave it the entire day. Make sure that the lid fits securely. Don't worry about it drying out as the meat gives off quite a bit of liquid while cooking, so it will stay moist. By dinnertime it will be ready! (If your hot tray has a heat level setting, set it on medium-high).

Serve with rice and peas.

SERVES 8–10

GLAZED CORN BEEF
and grainy mustard sauce

ALTHOUGH THIS PIECE OF MEAT IS ALREADY COOKED WHEN YOU GET IT FROM YOUR BUTCHER, IT DOESN'T STOP THERE! IT STILL LIKES TO BE BATHED, GLAZED AND PRAISED. AND PRAISE YOU WILL GET WHEN YOU SERVE IT!

1 x 2 kg cooked pickled hump
(ensure that you ask your butcher
to pickle and cook it)
1 x 470 g bottle hot chutney

FOR THE MUSTARD SAUCE
1 Tbsp mustard powder
1 Tbsp brown sugar
1 Tbsp cornflour
pinch salt
1 cup cold water
½ cup mayonnaise
1 Tbsp prepared, grainy mustard
½ cup non-dairy creamer

It's important to wash the hump well in cold running water to get rid of any excess salt from the pickling solution. Place it in a bowl, cover with boiling water and leave it to stand for about 15 minutes. Discard the water and rinse the meat again very well in cold water.

Preheat the oven to 160 °C. Place the hump into a deep ovenproof dish ensuring that there's not much space between the sides of the roasting dish and the meat – almost like 'one shoe size too big'. Cover the roast with three-quarters of the bottle of chutney (reserve one-quarter for a final basting before serving). You really want the meat to soak up and 'wallow' in the chutney while it's cooking.

Place a lid on the dish and bake, covered, for 1½ hours.

Remove the lid and pour the rest of the chutney over the top of the hump. Turn the heat up to 180 °C and allow it to bake for another 10–15 minutes or until it browns. Remove from the oven and serve with mustard sauce.

MUSTARD SAUCE:
Combine the mustard powder, sugar, cornflour, salt and cold water in a pot. Bring to the boil, remove from the heat and add the mayonnaise, grainy mustard and creamer. If you don't want it to be too thick, add a little more water. Mix well with a whisk and reheat when ready to serve.

Note: If you don't have a small, deep ovenproof dish, place one layer of aluminium foil vertically and another horizontally into a roasting pan. Place the meat in the centre of the foil, cover it with chutney, pull both pieces of foil up and seal it by twisting the foil in the middle.

SERVES 6–8

CRUNCHY CARAWAY CABBAGE AND BRISKET
on mash

THIS IS A FOUR-STEP RECIPE THAT MAY LOOK LIKE ONE OF THOSE RECIPES YOU'D LIKE SOMEBODY ELSE TO TRY FIRST BUT BELIEVE ME IT'S REALLY SIMPLE! THE TEXTURES AND FLAVOURS OF THIS FOUR-LAYERED DISH ARE WHAT MAKE IT UNIQUE. THE VELVETY SMOOTHNESS OF THE MASH WITH THE SWEET-AND-SOUR CRUNCH OF THE CABBAGE ALL WRAPPED UP IN THE BEEFY FLAVOUR OF BRISKET WITH A FINAL CRUNCH OF RYE CROUTONS IS JUST SOMETHING SPECIAL.

FOR THE CROUTONS (STEP ONE)
1 small loaf of rye bread
oil for frying

FOR THE MASHED POTATO (STEP TWO)
8 medium potatoes
2 Tbsp non-dairy margarine
2 Tbsp non-dairy creamer
salt and pepper

FOR THE CABBAGE (STEP THREE)
½ cup white vinegar
1 heaped Tbsp syrup
1 Tbsp sweet chilli sauce
1 Tbsp lemon juice
1 Tbsp brown sugar
½ head white cabbage, shredded (not as finely as coleslaw, but a little thicker)
½ cup sultanas (yellow raisins)
1 tsp caraway seeds (optional)
½ tsp salt
1 heaped Tbsp cornflour

CROUTONS:

Remove all the crusts and cut the bread into small cubes (smaller than bite size). Fry in hot oil until golden brown. The croutons brown quickly so fry a few at a time, turning constantly to acquire an even colour. When golden, place on brown paper to drain.

The croutons can be prepared in advance but should be kept at room temperature in an airtight container. They can even be made the day before.

MASHED POTATO:

Peel, cut up and boil the potatoes until soft. Strain off the excess water, add the margarine and creamer, and mash the potatoes. Add salt and pepper to taste and set aside until needed.

CABBAGE:

Place the vinegar, syrup, sweet chilli sauce, lemon juice and brown sugar into a large pot and heat on low heat until the syrup has melted.

Add the shredded cabbage and cook on medium to high heat for about 5 minutes, stirring continuously so that the cabbage becomes nicely coated with the sweet-and-sour sauce. The cabbage will make its own water as well. Don't cook the cabbage for more than 5–7 minutes as you don't want it to be too limp.

Add the sultanas, caraway seeds and salt to the cabbage and cook for a minute or two. Remove from the heat and leave it to stand in the pot, covered, for 10 minutes.

CONTINUED ON PAGE 70

FOR THE BRISKET (STEP FOUR)

2 x 500 g packets vacuum-
packed cooked or
smoked brisket

After 10 minutes drain the excess cabbage water into a small bowl and leave to cool.

Add the cornflour to the cooled cabbage juice, mix well and pour back over the cabbage. (It's difficult to determine how much water each cabbage makes so for every cup of juice drained, add a heaped tablespoon of cornflour.)

Place back on the stove and heat through just until the sauce thickens so that the cabbage looks glazed. Remove from the heat immediately and set aside.

BRISKET:

Bring a large pot of water to the boil (large enough to hold the two packets of brisket) and drop the packets into the water. Bring the water to the boil again, reduce the heat, and allow the bags to simmer on low heat for 10–15 minutes – this should be enough to heat it through.

TO ASSEMBLE:

Place the mashed potato (you may have to reheat it) on a large, flat, round serving dish or platter and spread evenly over the dish. The mash should be spooned slightly higher and thicker around the edges so that the cabbage sauce stays in the middle of the mash and doesn't leak out at the sides.

While the mash is being reheated either in the pot or in the microwave, reheat the cabbage. Place the hot cabbage in the middle of the mash.

Remove the meat from the hot water and slice open the bags. Separate the layers of meat and arrange loosely over the cabbage.

Sprinkle croutons on top of the meat and serve immediately.

SERVES 8

double-dunked
T-BONE STEAKS

DOUBLE THE EFFORT FOR DOUBLY DELICIOUS RESULTS!

4 T-bone steaks

FOR DUNK 1
2 cups red wine (500 ml)
1 tsp freshly grated garlic
1 tsp freshly grated ginger

FOR DUNK 2
The Butcher's Baster No. 1 on page 16

Place the steaks in a shallow, rectangular dish. Pour the wine, garlic and ginger over the T-bones. Marinate for 12–18 hours (no longer).

Remove the steaks from Dunk 1, draining off all the liquid, and place them into the Butcher's Baster. Allow to marinate the whole day or overnight.

Either braai/barbecue or fry and serve with baked potato if you can still fit anything else on the plate.

Tip: To know if your braai/barbecue is ready, place your hands about 10 cm above the grid/cooking tray and if you can count to four or five before you have to lift them, the braai/barbecue is ready for the meat!

SERVES 4

London broil
BEEFEATER LUNCH

WHENEVER I HEAR THE WORDS 'LONDON BROIL', I IMMEDIATELY CONJURE UP IMAGES OF RED BUSES AND BOBBIES ON THE BEAT. BUT FOR THIS RECIPE A MORE APPROPRIATE IMAGE WOULD BE THAT OF AN ENGLISH COUNTRYSIDE PUB WHERE THE SMELL OF BARRELLED BEER AND HEAVILY POLISHED WOOD HANGS IN THE AIR!

6 pieces London broil
1 x 375 ml bottle beer
(your favourite)
¼ cup Worcestershire sauce
1 tsp Hot English
mustard powder
½ cup tomato sauce

Place the London broil steaks side by side in an oblong glass dish and pour the whole bottle of beer over them. Allow to marinate the entire day. Just before cooking, remove the steaks and discard the beer.

Combine the Worcestershire sauce, mustard powder and tomato sauce. Paint or baste each steak with the sauce, making sure they are well coated. The steaks can either be fried in a ridged (lined) cast-iron steak pan or on a braai/barbecue. If using a skillet, make sure it's really hot so that the steaks smoke and sizzle as you put them in. Don't put more than two on a skillet at a time.

As the beads of blood appear on the upper sides of the steaks, turn the meat over and reduce the heat.

The best way to serve them is by fanning them, so while they are cooking, slice them at an angle across the run of the grain with a sharp knife, three-quarters of the way through at 1 cm intervals. This way you'll also be able to see how well done they are. If they aren't cooked through, allow them to cook for a little longer or place them in a preheated oven at 180 °C for a few minutes while you fry the rest of the steaks.

Note: For those who prefer not to marinate and baste their meat, dip them in a little oil and sprinkle with a braai spice. They will still taste great!

TO SERVE:
Eat it London pub-style on an open baguette with a spoon of English mustard and some hot fries on the side.

SERVES 6–8 DEPENDING ON THE SIZE OF THE CUTS

SCOTCH FILLET STEAK
with lashings of green garlic 'butter' or creamy mushroom sauce

THIS RECIPE BRINGS BACK WONDERFUL MEMORIES OF MY LATE FATHER WHO ALWAYS REQUESTED THAT HIS STEAK BE 'COVERED IN A CARPET OF GARLIC'. HE LOVED IT AND I FORTUNATELY (OR IS IT UNFORTUNATELY FOR OTHERS) INHERITED THAT LOVE TOO. GARLIC HAS THE MOST WONDERFUL ANTI-BACTERIAL PROPERTIES, BUT IT'S DIFFICULT CONVINCING THOSE WHO LOVE SHARING OTHER PASSIONS WITH YOU IF GARLIC IS JUST NOT THEIR THING!

8 Scotch fillet steaks, vacuum packed (Leave Scotch fillet steaks in your fridge for 7–10 days. If you don't use them after 10 days, place them in the freezer.)

FOR THE MARINADE
½ cup oil
2 Tbsp Worcestershire sauce
2 Tbsp soy sauce
2 Tbsp brown sugar
1 tsp crushed garlic
½ cup red wine

FOR THE GREEN GARLIC 'BUTTER'
½ cup non-dairy margarine
½ cup non-dairy creamer
2 tsp crushed garlic
¼ tsp salt
1 Tbsp cornflour dissolved in ½ cup cold water
2 Tbsp finely chopped fresh parsley

Remove the steaks from their vacuum bags the day you require them and marinate for a few hours in the marinade.

MARINADE:
Combine all the ingredients.

FRYING THE STEAKS:
When ready to cook, remove the meat from the marinade and grill on a very hot skillet to brown and seal the outsides. Cook as you prefer – underdone, medium or well done. Remove the steaks from the pan and leave to rest in a dish covered with aluminium foil.
   Don't wash the frying pan just yet, as you need it for the mushroom sauce.

GREEN GARLIC 'BUTTER':
Melt the margarine in a small pot. When melted, remove from the heat. Add the rest of the ingredients, stirring or whisking as you do. Place back onto the heat and keep stirring until it starts to simmer. Switch off the heat and leave the sauce to absorb all the flavours. Reheat when ready to serve.

CONTINUED ON PAGE 78

FOR THE MUSHROOM SAUCE

1 mushroom stock cube

1½ cups boiling water

250 g button mushrooms

250 g small black
mushrooms, sliced

250 g large black
mushrooms, sliced

1 Tbsp non-dairy margarine

½ cup white wine (optional, but
when serving adults, add it!)

2 level Tbsp cornflour

1 cup non-dairy creamer

salt and ground black pepper

MUSHROOM SAUCE:

And for those who can't quite appreciate garlic's wonderful anti-bacterial properties, here's a 'creamy' alternative! 'There's no way this mushroom sauce doesn't have cream in it, it's just too creamy,' a friend of mine remarked indignantly. So, to prove him wrong, this one's for you, Mark!

Dissolve the mushroom stock cube in the boiling water and place in the fridge to cool. Fry all the mushrooms in the margarine (in the pan used to fry the steaks). When the mushrooms start to give off their own liquid, add the wine and bring to the boil. Simmer for a few minutes.

Meanwhile dissolve the cornflour in the creamer and cooled mushroom stock and add to the simmering mushrooms. Bring to the boil, allowing the mixture to thicken. Add salt and ground black pepper to taste. Switch off the heat and reheat when ready to serve.

Note: Serve with any one of the potato dishes on pages 175–177. Mash goes down very well!

Tip: Try to avoid cutting into a steak to see if it is cooked. Press into it with tongs instead – cooked meat will offer some resistance and spring back.

SERVES 8

big five
'MOCK T-BONES' AT THEIR BEST

FOR ME, ONE OF THE HIGHLIGHTS OF A GAME RESERVE HOLIDAY IS THE EVENING BRAAI/BARBECUE. EVERYBODY IS HUNGRY, BUT THE TRANQUILLITY OF THE PARK, ABSORBED BY ALL WHO ENTER IT, SOMEHOW ENABLES EVEN CHILDREN TO ACCEPT THAT THERE WILL BE DELAYS IN PREPARING MEALS! THE IMMEDIACIES AND URGENCIES OF LIFE REMAIN AT THE GATES UPON ENTERING THE PARK, UNFORTUNATELY ONLY TO BE RETRIEVED UPON EXITING!

TRADITIONALLY, ALL MEALS 'HAVE TO CONTAIN MEAT' IN THE PARK – SO IT'S NORMALLY A BIG MACON AND SAUSAGE FRY-UP FOR BREAKFAST, COLD MEAT BAGELS FOR LUNCH AND, NATURALLY, STEAK AND WORS FOR DINNER!

SO WHY ARE THEY CALLED 'BIG 5' MOCK T-BONES? WELL, BECAUSE ONLY FIVE INGREDIENTS ARE USED IN THE MARINADE. AND YOU THOUGHT IT HAD SOMETHING TO DO WITH THE ANIMALS!

1 cup red wine (or Shabbat wine)
1 cup chutney (mild or hot)
1 cup tomato sauce
1 tsp crushed garlic
½ cup Worcestershire sauce
8 blade steaks on the bone,
cut 1.5 cm thick (or thicker if
you prefer)

The night before you are going to eat these, combine the ingredients and pour over the meat. Refrigerate until needed.
I usually allow mine to marinate overnight but you could do it in the morning before you go out into the park and cook it that night.

Tip: A tip that I once got from a fellow camper went as follows: 'Each man standing around the braai should pour a little beer from his can over the steaks while they're cooking – a man needs to mark his territory, you know,' he said. So with that in mind I hope you have a 'pee'ceful sleep and that you see all five on your next visit.

SERVES 6–8

ANNA'S PORTUGUESE KEBABS
with dirty rice

WHILE AT COLLEGE MANY YEARS AGO, I BEFRIENDED A BEAUTIFUL GIRL FROM MOZAMBIQUE. HER MOM COOKED TRADITIONAL SPICY PORTUGUESE FOOD AND THE AROMA FROM HER KITCHEN WHEN COOKING WAS STRONG ENOUGH TO MAKE YOU HUNGRY BUT DIDN'T LEAVE YOUR CLOTHES SMELLING OF PERI-PERI OR YOUR HAIR OF GARLIC.

8 beef kebabs

FOR THE MARINADE
5 cloves garlic
3 red chillies (the tiny hot ones!), seeded
2 tsp lemon juice
1 Tbsp tomato paste
2 tsp brown sugar
¼ cup dry white wine
½ cup olive oil

FOR THE DIRTY RICE
200 g grilled chicken livers (obtainable at most butcheries)
1½ cups uncooked rice
1 tsp turmeric
1 tsp paprika
2 Tbsp peri-peri sauce (any one of your favourites)
1 tsp crushed garlic
1 Tbsp tomato paste
2 Tbsp onion soup powder
salt and pepper
4 cups chicken stock (2 chicken stock cubes dissolved in 4 cups boiling water)

MARINADE:
Blend all the ingredients together with a hand blender or in a food processor. Place the kebabs side by side in a flat glass dish and cover with the marinade. Leave to marinate overnight.

DIRTY RICE:
Preheat the oven to 180 °C. Wash the livers well and cut them into quarters. Place them in a deep ovenproof dish. Wash the rice then spread it out on top of the livers. Sprinkle the rest of the dry ingredients on top of the rice. Pour the chicken stock over the rice and give it all a good stir. Place in the oven for 45 minutes. Reduce the heat to 140 °C and cook for a further 30 minutes.

TO SERVE:
The kebabs can either be fried in a pan coated with a little non-stick cooking spray or placed on the braai/barbecue. Serve with Dirty Rice.

Notes: Ask your butcher to make the kebabs out of side bolo OR ask him for cubed beef and thread them yourself. There are some wonderful extra-long sticks available in most supermarkets. There are also specially designed stainless steel rods for Espatados.
Dirty Rice can be made in the morning and refrigerated, but I wouldn't refrigerate it for more than about 12 hours as it contains liver.

SERVES 4–6

CHOLENT
a Shabbos event

MY CHILDREN MAINTAIN THAT CHOLENT (TRADITIONAL ALL-NIGHT STEW) NEEDS TO BE 'EATEN WITH A CROWD AND DIGESTED ALONE' AND THEY'RE CONVINCED THAT THAT'S HOW THE 'SHABBOS SHLOFF/SLEEP' CAME ABOUT. AFTER EATING CHOLENT YOU NEED TO 'WIND' DOWN!

CHOLENT IS ONE OF THE MOST ANCIENT AND BEST-PRESERVED JEWISH FOODS BORN OUT OF THE OBSERVANCE OF THE SABBATH. FIRES CANNOT BE KINDLED AND COOKING IS PROHIBITED DURING THE SABBATH. THEREFORE, CHOLENT HAS TO BE MADE ON FRIDAY AFTERNOON (BEFORE THE SABBATH COMES IN) AND COOKED UNINTERRUPTED IN AN OVEN OR CROCKPOT UNTIL THE FOLLOWING DAY WHEN IT IS SERVED FOR LUNCH. THE FUN THING ABOUT CHOLENT IS THAT OVER THE YEARS AS THE JEWISH PEOPLE HAVE MIGRATED TO DIFFERENT PARTS OF THE WORLD, THEY HAVE ADOPTED THAT COUNTRY'S FOODS AND MODIFIED IT ACCORDINGLY. WE PUT SAMP MEALIES IN OURS! OUR FRIEND MICKEY, WHO'S OF MOROCCAN DESCENT, PUTS COUSCOUS IN HIS! AS A RESULT WE HAVE MANY DIFFERENT ETHNICALLY-INFLUENCED CHOLENT RECIPES.

CHOLENT IS A VERY FORGIVING DISH AND YOU CAN EXPERIMENT TO FIND THE RIGHT ONE FOR YOU. HERE IS THE 'START-UP PACK' FOR BEEF CHOLENT. CHANGE IT AS YOU PLEASE AND BECOME YOUR OWN CHOLENT QUEEN. LAMB IS ALSO DELICIOUS WITH A TABLESPOON OF CURRY POWDER AND A TIN OF CURRIED VEGETABLES ADDED TO IT.

½ cup barley

½ cup sugar beans

½ cup small white beans

½ cup samp

2 slices top rib

2 slices blade steak

1 piece meaty shin

3 marrow bones (or more if Gary Cohen is coming!)

2 beef stock cubes dissolved in 3 cups boiling water

1 onion, chopped

4 large carrots, chopped or sliced into rounds

½ tsp freshly crushed garlic

2 sticks celery, chopped

6 potatoes, peeled and cut in half

2 Tbsp tomato paste (available in sealed packets)

3 Tbsp onion soup powder

2 Tbsp chicken stock powder

salt and pepper

(You may need to add more liquid to the cholent to cover the ingredients.)

Soak the barley, beans and samp in water overnight. The following morning wash them and ensure there are no insects floating around. Leave them to soak in fresh water until you are ready to use them.

I normally start preparing my cholent early Friday afternoon. Slice the top rib into smaller pieces, and fry until brown on both sides. In the same pan fry the blade steak, shin and marrow bones on both sides until brown. Take your time browning the meat as this makes all the difference to the final colour.

As you finish browning the pieces of meat, place them straight into the crockpot or slow cooker. Add the beef stock to the pan in which the meat was browning and scrape up all the bits of meat off the bottom, bring to the boil and then pour this liquid over the meat.

Place the onion, carrots, garlic and celery on top of the meat in the crockpot, followed by the drained barley, beans and samp, the potatoes, tomato paste, onion soup and chicken stock powders. Add salt and pepper to taste. The meat and vegetables should be totally covered with water as the beans and barley absorb quite a bit of the liquid. Give everything a good stir and say good night to it. Don't touch it, don't think about it, and don't even look at it until you lift the lid off to serve it for lunch the next day.

Note: When ordering blade steak, ask your butcher to cut it in half through the bone.

Tip: My friend Leigh was her apartment block's Cholent Queen (admittedly there were only four apartments in her block!), but everybody in her building knew that it was Shabbos when the aroma of her cholent started permeating through the walls! This was her tip: Place 1 x 200 g packet of 'boil in the bag' rice down the side of the cholent. The tiny holes in the cooking bag allow it to absorb all the flavours of the cholent. Place a potato or two on top of the bag otherwise it tends to float up to the surface leaving some rice uncooked.

SERVES MANY

OSSO BUCO

SHIN ALWAYS SEEMED TO HAVE THE STIGMA OF 'SOUP MEAT' ATTACHED TO IT AND NEEDED TO BE UPGRADED TO ITS HIGHLY RESPECTED POSITION IN ITALIAN CUISINE AS OSSO BUCO OR HOLLOW-BONED BEEF. THE WONDERFUL FLAVOUR IMPARTED BY THE BONE MARROW IS A SPECIAL TREAT! TRADITIONALLY, OSSO BUCO IS SERVED WITH GREMOLATA (SEE BELOW), WHICH IS ADDED TO THE DISH AT THE VERY END.

¾ cup flour
¼ cup gravy powder
6 slices beef shin (when ordering the meat, tell your butcher you need meaty pieces for osso buco)
oil for frying
1 cup red wine
1 chicken stock cube dissolved in 1 cup boiling water
1 cup tomato cocktail juice
1½ cups chopped onion
½ cup chopped celery
1½ cups sliced or chopped carrots
½ cup chopped fresh Italian parsley
½ tsp grated fresh ginger
1 tsp crushed garlic
1 heaped Tbsp chopped fresh thyme (or ½ tsp dried)
2 heaped Tbsp chopped fresh basil (or ½ tsp dried)
1 x 410 g tin peeled and chopped tomatoes
1 Tbsp brown sugar
salt and pepper

FOR THE GREMOLATA (OPTIONAL)
2 Tbsp chopped fresh parsley
2 tsp minced garlic
1 tsp finely grated lemon zest

Combine the flour and gravy powder and coat each piece of meat with the mixture.

Brown the meat in a little oil, but don't let it burn as you need to add wine and stock to the pan once you have removed the meat. When brown, remove from the pan and place the meat in an ovenproof dish.

Using the same pan as for the meat, add the wine, chicken stock and tomato cocktail juice. Bring to the boil and leave it to simmer for 5 minutes, then remove from the heat and pour over the meat.

Preheat the oven to 180 °C. In the same pan used to fry the meat, add a little more oil and fry the onion, celery, carrots, parsley, ginger, garlic, thyme and basil. Cook for about 10 minutes, then add the tomatoes, brown sugar, salt and pepper to taste, and mix until the sugar has dissolved.

Pour this over the meat, mix well, cover and place in the oven for 1 hour.

Reduce the heat to 160 °C, stir and cook for another hour.

Remove the lid and cook the meat for about 30 minutes, basting every now and then. If you find that there is not enough moisture, add a little more chicken stock. If you feel there's a little too much liquid, leave the meat in the oven, uncovered, basting it to keep it moist but allowing the liquid to evaporate a little and reduce.

GREMOLATA:
About 10 minutes before serving, sprinkle the gremolata over the osso buco and gently stir it into the gravy.

SERVES 6

OLD-FASHIONED STEAK PIE
with minted peas

IF THERE IS ONE PERSON WHO CAN MAKE STEAK PIE, IT'S MY FRIEND BEV. THIS IS A HEARTY GRAVY-FILLED PIE WITH A DELICIOUS FLAVOUR THAT ALWAYS TASTES LIKE 'THE GOOD OLD DAYS'. WHEN I ASKED HER FOR THE RECIPE ONE DAY, SHE BURST OUT LAUGHING SAYING, 'THIS IS YOUR MOTHER'S RECIPE THAT YOU GAVE ME!'

½ cup flour
2 Tbsp gravy powder
1 kg cubed steak
2 onions, chopped
little oil for frying
2 beef stock cubes dissolved in
3 cups boiling water
salt and pepper
1 x 400 g puff pastry

FOR THE MINTED PEAS
½ x 500 g packet frozen peas
3–4 mint leaves
½ tsp salt
1 tsp sugar

Sift the flour and gravy powder over the steak cubes, mixing it all together until each piece is coated.

Fry the chopped onions in a large pot in a little oil until dark brown (the secret to steak pie is ensuring that the onions are golden brown in colour, but not burnt). Remove the onions and set aside.

Add a little more oil to the same pot and fry small batches of cubed steak until brown. Repeat until you've cooked all the meat. Set the meat aside.

Add the beef stock to the same pot and stir well, scraping all the brown bits off the bottom. Place the meat and onions back into the pot, cover and leave to simmer on low for 35–40 minutes, stirring every now and then. The gravy should not be watery and should thicken as it boils and reduces. Add salt and pepper to taste. Switch the stove off and leave the meat to rest in the gravy and cool slightly.

Preheat the oven to 200 °C. On a lightly floured surface, unroll the pastry and gently smooth it out with a rolling pin. Don't roll it out too thinly. Place the pie dish you're going to use upside down on the pastry and cut out a pastry lid. Lift the dish off the pastry and fill it with meat and gravy. Wet the rim of the dish with water and cover the meat with the pre-cut pastry lid. Press the pastry against the sides of the pie dish. Bake in the oven for 30–40 minutes or until golden brown.

MINTED PEAS:
Boil the peas and mint leaves in salted and sugared water. As the peas start to boil, switch the stove off and cover the pot with a lid so that the peas can absorb the minty flavour for 5–10 minutes. Bring to the boil again just before serving.

SERVES 4–6

Mr Reddy's CURRY

EVERY TIME I SMELL FRESH CORIANDER IT TAKES ME BACK TO MY CHILDHOOD AND REMINDS ME OF MR REDDY, WHO WORKED FOR MY PARENTS FOR MANY YEARS AND COOKED CURRY EVERY DAY FOR LUNCH. EVERYTHING HE USED IN HIS CURRY WAS FRESH, DIRECT FROM HIS HOME-GROWN CHILLI BUSH AND HERB GARDEN. HIS FAVOURITE SAYING WAS, 'NEVER BE IN A HURRY OR YOU'LL SPOIL YOUR CURRY.' SO WITH PATIENCE AND ENTHUSIASM WE WOULD OFTEN WATCH HIM PREPARE HIS DELICIOUS CURRY, WHICH FOR THREE GENERATIONS WE HAVE CONTINUED TO ENJOY!

little oil for frying
1.5 kg cubed beef/lamb, off the bone
1 large onion, chopped
1 heaped tsp crushed garlic
3 red hot chillies, seeded and chopped
1 Tbsp hot curry powder
±12 curry leaves
½ cup finely chopped fresh coriander
1 heaped tsp finely grated fresh ginger
3 carrots, sliced
3 red tomatoes, seeded and chopped
1 Tbsp apricot jam
4 large potatoes, cubed
1 stick cinnamon
salt and pepper
2 cups water

Heat the oil in a large saucepan and brown the meat in small batches. Allow the meat to brown (but not burn) as this helps to create a dark base for the curry. Once all the meat has been fried, add a little more oil to the pot and fry the onion, garlic, chillies and curry powder. Sauté for a few minutes, then add the curry leaves, coriander, ginger, carrots, tomatoes, jam, potatoes, cinnamon, and salt and pepper to taste. Add the water and stir well.

Leave to simmer on the top of the stove, covered, for at least 1–1½ hours until the meat is tender. Alternatively, once the water has been added and brought to the boil, transfer the curry to an ovenproof dish and cook it, covered, in the oven at 170 °C for 1½–2 hours.

Note: Another thing I do remember about Mr Reddy's curry was that it was always accompanied by a chopped banana and hot achar (mixed pickles), straight from the bottle!

Tip: Never allow a casserole or curry to boil rapidly as this will toughen the meat.

SERVES 8

good old-fashioned RECIPE FOR STIR-FRY

MY MIDDLE SON, DARREN, COULD LIVE ON STIR-FRY, SO WE'VE TRIED AND TESTED MANY RECIPES, BUT THIS IS THE ONE THAT ALWAYS GETS THE RED ROSETTE!

1 Tbsp peri-peri oil
1 kg beef/chicken stir-fry meat
1 x 750 g packet ready-cut, *fresh* stir-fry vegetables
1 x 250 g packet shredded cabbage and carrots
toasted sesame seeds and/or cashew nuts

FOR THE SAUCE
½ cup soy sauce
1 heaped Tbsp cornflour dissolved in 1 cup cold water
1 tsp grated fresh ginger
1 tsp crushed garlic
1 Tbsp vinegar
1 heaped Tbsp brown sugar
1 tsp peanut butter
2 Tbsp sweet chilli sauce
1 tsp hot chilli sauce

SAUCE:
Combine all the sauce ingredients, mix well and set aside.

STIR-FRY:
Heat the peri-peri oil in a frying pan or wok. Fry the beef/chicken in small batches – too much meat will boil rather than brown.

When cooked (not too long, as chicken cooks quickly), remove and set aside. Pour the sauce over the cooked meat and mix well.

Fry the vegetables, underdone rather than overdone, as they should be crunchy and, since they are going to be placed back into the pan to be heated through, they just need a minute or two the first time around. Add the vegetables to the marinating meat and toss it all together so that the vegetables also become coated in sauce.

Reheat everything in the pan just before serving. The sauce should also thicken slightly and form a light glaze over the stir-fry. Sprinkle with toasted sesame seeds and/or cashew nuts. To toast the seeds and/nuts, place under the grill for 1 minute, but keep a close watch as they burn quickly. (When grilling in an electric oven, the door should be left slightly ajar to keep the element red. However, when using a gas oven, this is not the case and it should be left closed.)

Note: If ready-cut, fresh stir-fry vegetables are unavailable use frozen vegetables or slice up onions, green beans, baby corn, shredded cabbage, carrots, baby marrows and different-coloured peppers.

Tips: It's easier to slice meat into thin slices while it's still slightly frozen, or get your butcher to do it for you!

Meat should be cooked separately from vegetables when stir-frying. When ready to serve, combine the two and heat through.

SERVES 4–6

BOOZY BEEF
and the Sunday papers

THERE'S NOTHING BETTER THAN RELAXING ON A COLD DAY WITH THE FIRE BURNING, NEWSPAPERS SPREAD ACROSS THE FLOOR, EATING A HEARTY BEEF DISH THAT HAS BEEN COOKING SLOWLY FOR HOURS IN A DARK RICH GRAVY.

3 leeks, sliced
4 large carrots, sliced
2 onions, chopped
little oil for frying
1.5 kg beef stroganoff strips
½ cup flour mixed with
1 Tbsp gravy powder and
1 tsp mustard powder
1 cup beer
2 cups beef stock (2 beef stock cubes mixed with 2 cups boiling water)
1 x 115 g tin tomato paste
1 tsp brown sugar
salt and pepper

Fry the vegetables in a little oil until limp. Remove and set aside.

Sprinkle the meat with the flour mixture and fry in the same pot used for the vegetables. Fry a little at a time so that the meat browns (too much meat will cause it to boil). Once all the meat has been fried, put it all back into the pot and add the beer and beef stock. Place the vegetables back into the pot with the meat and simmer for about 10 minutes. If you are using a large cast-iron pot, which is also suitable for the oven, place it, covered, into the oven at 160 °C for 1 hour. Otherwise, transfer the meat into an ovenproof dish, cover it with foil or a lid, and do the same.

Remove the meat from the oven and add the tomato purée, sugar, and salt and pepper to taste. Stir well and if at this point you feel there isn't enough liquid, add a little water. It really depends on how you like your gravy – thicker or thinner! Turn the oven down to 140 °C and cook for a further 1 hour.

Note: The best part of this meal is using a chunk of bread to soak up all the gravy!

SERVES 6–8

MARCO'S MOM'S BEEF STRIPS
with basil dumplings

OUR FRIEND MARCO'S MOTHER WAS A SUPERB COOK, A REAL MAMA IN THE KITCHEN, KNOWN FOR HER CULINARY SKILLS, ESPECIALLY WHEN IT CAME TO MEAT. THIS DISH WAS HER SPECIALITY AND SHE MADE IT FOR EVERY FAMILY FUNCTION WHETHER ASKED TO OR NOT! NOBODY DARED TO SUGGEST OTHERWISE, AFTER ALL 'IT WAS THE ONLY THING MARCO'S PAPA WOULD EAT' OR SO SHE TOLD HIM! SO WE MADE A DEAL ONE DAY. SHE ALLOWED ME TO WATCH HER MAKE HER FAMOUS DISH AND I HAD TO GIVE HER A PLATTER OF CHOPPED LIVER! WHAT SHE FORGOT TO MENTION WAS THAT HER PART OF THE DEAL WAS A ONCE OFF AND MINE WAS 'WHENEVER SHE WANTED IT!'

±10 baby onions, peeled and cut in half
little oil for frying
3 sticks celery, sliced
2 heaped Tbsp finely chopped fresh basil (or 1 tsp dried)
2 Tbsp roughly chopped fresh parsley (or 1 tsp dried)
1 tsp crushed garlic
1 x 250 g punnet mushrooms, sliced
1 kg beef stroganoff strips
½ cup flour mixed with
1 Tbsp gravy powder and
1 tsp mustard powder
2 chicken stock cubes dissolved in 4 cups boiling water (reserve 1 cup to be added later with the dumplings)
1 cup tomato cocktail juice
1 x 410 g tin Italian sliced tomatoes with origanum and basil
1 Tbsp brown sugar
1 x 410 g tin butter beans

Preheat the oven to 180 °C. Fry the baby onions in a little oil until lightly browned on the outside.

Add the celery, basil, parsley and garlic and sauté for about 5 minutes. Add the mushrooms and, once most of the water from the mushrooms has evaporated, remove the vegetables from the heat and place into a deep ovenproof dish. Make sure the dish is deep and large as the meat and dumplings still have to be added.

Dust the stroganoff strips with the flour, gravy and mustard mixture. Add a little oil to the same pot the vegetables were fried in and start browning the meat. Brown a few strips at a time so that they brown and don't boil. Remove the meat from the pan and place on top of the vegetables in the ovenproof dish.

To the same pot in which the meat was browned, add 3 cups of stock, the tomato cocktail juice, Italian sliced tomatoes, sugar and butter beans. Bring to the boil and pour over the meat.

Cover with a lid or aluminium foil and place in the oven for 40 minutes. While the meat is cooking, make the dumplings.

FOR THE DUMPLINGS

1 large onion, finely chopped
or grated

2 Tbsp non-dairy margarine

2 heaped Tbsp chopped fresh
basil leaves

1½ cups sifted flour

2 tsp baking powder

salt and pepper

2 cups water

DUMPLINGS:

Fry the onion in the margarine until glassy. Add the basil and cook for a further 5 minutes, then remove from the heat and set aside.

Place the sifted flour, baking powder, salt and pepper into a plastic bowl. Make a well in the centre and place the onions and basil in the middle. Start by adding 1½ cups of water, mixing it with a wooden spoon to form a soft dough, which should be slightly sticky but pliable enough to roll into golf ball-sized balls. Add the last ½ cup water slowly while you mix as you may not need it all. Dipping your hands into water before rolling the dough makes it a little easier to form the balls.

Remove the meat from the oven after 40 minutes, add the 1 cup chicken stock set aside earlier, and stir well. Place the balls into the gravy, pushing them around a bit until they are covered. Don't worry if the tops are peeping out! 'Don't be nervous,' Marco's mom told me, 'a confident cook makes people want to eat her food, 'cause they're too nervous not to.' If you feel the gravy is a little too thick, add a little more water. Water evaporation always depends on the length and width of your roasting pan/dish. For this reason I prefer a deep roasting dish when making this recipe. Cover the meat with a lid or aluminium foil.

Place the meat and dumplings back into the oven for a further 30 minutes. 'Don't peep for 30 minutes as the dumplings won't rise nicely,' said Marco's mother. And we think we're superstitious!

Turn the oven down to 160 °C and leave the dish to cook for a further 30 minutes. Taste a piece of beef to see if it is soft enough. If not, leave it in for a little longer until tender.

Serve with peas and boiled baby potatoes. Mashed potatoes also work well.

SERVES 6

Mexican
FIESTA

A FEW YEARS AGO WE SWAPPED TIMESHARE FOR A RESORT IN MEXICO AND PART OF THE ENTERTAINMENT WAS DAILY COOKING DEMONSTRATIONS. NATURALLY, I COULDN'T WAIT TO GET HOME TO RECREATE A MEXICAN FIESTA. IF YOU DON'T FEEL LIKE MAKING THE SALSA AND GUACAMOLE, BUY IT – IT WILL STILL BE GREAT. AFTER TWO MARGARITAS, WHO'LL KNOW THE DIFFERENCE ANYWAY!

FOR THE REFRIED BEANS
KOSHER-STYLE
1 large onion, finely chopped
250 g beef macon, finely chopped (optional)
little oil for frying
1 clove garlic, crushed
½ tsp cumin powder
1 x 420 g tin baked beans in tomato sauce
salt and black pepper

FOR THE GUACAMOLE
3 ripe avocados
4 cloves fresh garlic
2 Tbsp lime or lemon juice
1 tsp salt
1 tsp crushed black pepper
2 Tbsp tangy mayonnaise

REFRIED BEANS:
This should be made before frying the meat for the fajitas, then reheated.

  Fry the onion and macon in a little oil until the onion is brown. Add the garlic, cumin and baked beans. Season with salt and pepper. Leave to simmer for a few minutes and, while simmering, mash with a potato masher a few times here and there – it must still remain lumpy and bumpy!

Before frying the meat for the fajitas make up the guacamole and salsa as per the recipes below and refrigerate. This can be done in the morning for that same evening, but not the day before, as the avocado will discolour.

GUACAMOLE:
Either mash or blend all the guacamole ingredients.

CONTINUED ON PAGE 96

FOR THE TOMATO SALSA

1 tsp sugar

½ cup lime or lemon juice

1 tsp salt

3 tomatoes, chopped

1 large onion, chopped

1 bunch fresh coriander (35 g), finely chopped

FOR THE BEEF/CHICKEN FAJITAS

¼ cup fresh lime juice (use lemon juice if no limes are available)

½ cup oil

1 Tbsp brown sugar

2 red peppers (sweet, long jalapeños), cut in half, seeded and sliced

1 tsp crushed garlic

1 tsp Mexican spice powder (Robertson's™)

ground salt and black pepper

1 kg beef or chicken, cut stir-fry style

6 flour tortillas (as per recipe opposite) or laffas

TOMATO SALSA:

Combine the sugar, lime or lemon juice and salt in a bowl.

When the sugar and salt have dissolved in the juice, add the tomatoes, onion and coriander, combining well. Place in the fridge until needed.

BEEF/CHICKEN FAJITAS (PRONOUNCED FAH-HEE-TUHS):

These are delicately spiced pieces of meat/chicken/vegetables rolled up in tortilla (flat bread). The closest kosher version to this in South Africa is the laffa from Friends Bakery.

Combine the lime juice, oil, brown sugar, peppers, garlic, Mexican spice, salt and black pepper, pour over the meat and marinate for 2–3 hours.

Start frying the meat just before you're about to eat. Heat a heavy-based pot or frying pan and fry the meat a few strips at a time.

While the last batch is frying, heat up the beans again, either on the stove or in the microwave.

As you finish frying the last batch of meat, place all the fried meat back into the pan to heat it all through and serve it immediately with the refried beans, the salsa, guacamole and tortillas/laffas.

FOR THE FLOUR TORTILLAS

2 cups flour

1 heaped tsp baking powder

½ tsp salt

¼ cup oil

¾ cup water

FOR THE PINEAPPLE
MARGARITAS

1 large pineapple, peeled and
cut into chunks

juice of 2 limes or 1 lemon

2 cups ice cubes

½ cup tequila (taste the
margarita for strength – you may
want more tequila!)

FLOUR TORTILLAS:

The actual meaning of the word tortilla is 'omelette', and just as an omelette wraps around a filling, so does a tortilla.

Sift the flour, baking powder and salt into a mixing bowl. Make a well in the middle. Pour the oil and water into the well and mix everything together. You may need to add a little more water if the dough is too dry, but only a little bit at a time.

Turn the dough out onto a floured board and begin kneading until it is smooth.

Divide the dough and roll into balls, a little smaller than golf balls. Leave them to relax for about 10 minutes. Roll them out on a floured surface into thin flat circles.

On the stove, heat a non-stick frying pan on medium to high heat. Fry the tortillas one at a time and when bubbles start appearing on the upper side, turn it over. It should have lightly browned spots here and there on both sides when ready.

While one is cooking, roll out another one. They do cook quite quickly so don't forget about the one in the pan.

PINEAPPLE MARGARITAS:

Peel and cut the pineapple beforehand and keep it covered until you're ready to serve the drinks.

Place all the ingredients into a liquidiser with metal blades and blend for about 1 minute or until smooth.

SERVES 6

tri-coloured
PEPPERS AND SESAME BEEF

THIS RECIPE BRINGS BACK WARM, HUMOROUS CHILDHOOD MEMORIES OF MY PARENTS' 'CHINESE PHASE'. CHINESE COOKING WAS REALLY BIG, IN FACT, IT WAS SO BIG IN OUR HOME THAT MY FATHER HAD TO BUY A CANTEEN OF CHINESE CROCKERY JUST TO MAKE SURE THAT IT WOULDN'T ONLY TASTE AUTHENTIC BUT LOOK IT TOO! MY MOTHER GOT A 'SPECIAL RECIPE' FROM HER FAVOURITE RESTAURANT AT THE TIME AND THIS IS IT!

2 onions, sliced into eighths (separate each leaf)
1 yellow pepper, cut into thin strips lengthwise
1 red pepper, cut into thin strips lengthwise
1 green pepper, cut into thin strips lengthwise
1 tsp chopped garlic
2 tsp finely grated fresh ginger
1 Tbsp red wine vinegar
1 tsp brown sugar
1 Tbsp sweet chilli sauce
1 Tbsp chicken stock powder or 1 cube, crumbled
¼ cup soy sauce
1 Tbsp cornflour
1½ cups cold water
1 kg beef strips, cut stir-fry style
little oil for frying
½ cup sesame seeds

Fry the onions and peppers until soft. Add the garlic and ginger, and fry together for a further 3–4 minutes. Remove the vegetables and set aside.

In a glass bowl combine the vinegar, brown sugar, sweet chilli sauce, chicken stock powder or stock cube, soy sauce, cornflour and water, and set aside.

Fry the meat in small batches in a little oil until brown. As the strips are cooked, remove them from the pan and place them on top of the onions and peppers.

Once you have fried all the meat, stir the sauce mixture you set aside earlier and place into the same pan. Heat slowly until the sauce thickens.

Return the vegetables and meat to the sauce, combine well and heat through.

I serve mine with an option of angel's hair pasta or jasmine rice (for family members who eat gluten-free food). Cook the pasta or rice as per the instructions on the packet.

Sprinkle the meat with sesame seeds.

Tip: Don't overcrowd your wok or frying pan, which should be very hot when stir-frying. Rather fry little bits of meat or vegetables at a time – using too much meat or vegetables at once could cause them to boil rather than brown.

SERVES 6

marvellous
MINCE

Mince is one of my all-time favourites. There is so much you can do with mince.

When making beef burger patties or meatballs, remember you need a bit of natural beef fat in the meat otherwise they will be as hard as rocks! A little bit of fat also gives a lovely flavour. However, when making Bolognaise sauce, I cook the mince meat up first, place it in a strainer and pour boiling water over it to wash off all the fat, then place it back in the pot and flavour it.

Mince goes off very quickly, so if you're not going to use it the same day, freeze it. To defrost, place the mince in the fridge as it must stay cold. One should never defrost meat then refreeze it in its raw state. Defrost it, cook it and then freeze it. Cooked mince actually lasts for about 4 or 5 days in the fridge.

Never partially cook a beef patty to reheat later!

All meat shrinks in size when it is cooked and mince shrinks even more when it is cooked on a high temperature. Cooking mince at a moderate temperature will prevent extra shrinkage and retain the moisture. Overcooking causes moisture and fats to be drawn out of the meat making it very dry and tasteless.

curried meat
PHYLLO BLINTZES

THESE ARE WONDERFUL SERVED AS A STARTER WITH A MILD CHUTNEY DIP.

250 g minced meat
2 Tbsp peri-peri oil
1 x 410 g tin chakalaka
(mild, medium or hot –
whichever you prefer)
2 Tbsp tomato sauce
1 Tbsp finely chopped fresh
parsley or 1 tsp dried parsley
salt and pepper
1 x 500 g box phyllo pastry
oil for brushing

Fry the minced meat in the peri-peri oil, mixing well as you do so.

Add the chakalaka, tomato sauce, parsley, salt and pepper to taste, and stir continuously until heated through.

Remove from the heat and leave to cool.

Preheat the oven to 180 °C. Cut the phyllo sheets into squares by dividing each sheet into quarters. Keep the pastry you're not working with covered, as it dries out very quickly. Paint or spray each square with oil and use one square of pastry at a time.

Place 1 Tbsp mince on the top third of the square. Spread it out a little. Fold in the sides so that the meat doesn't fall out and roll up the pastry.

Bake in the oven for approximately 10 minutes or until golden brown. Serve with a mild fruity chutney.

MAKES ±25

my comfort PIE

WHAT IS COMFORT FOOD? IS IT SOMETHING THAT GIVES US A SENSE OF WELL-BEING, REMINDING US OF OUR CHILDHOOD AND HOME COOKING? IS IT A FEEL-GOOD MEAL THAT WARMS OUR HEARTS AND SATISFIES OUR EVERY NEED? OR IS IT SOMETHING WE ALWAYS BREAK OUR DIETS ON? COTTAGE PIE SEEMS TO COVER MOST OF THAT FOR MY FAMILY. IT EVEN SOUNDS COMFORTING, CUDDLY, COTTAGEY AND HOMELY.

6 large potatoes
1 Tbsp non-dairy margarine
½ cup non-dairy creamer
salt and pepper
2 cups beef stock
(2 beef stock cubes dissolved in 2 cups boiling water)
2 onions, chopped
oil for frying
1 tsp crushed garlic
2 carrots, grated
1 kg minced meat
1 x 115 g tin tomato paste
2 Tbsp gravy powder
1 tsp dried mixed herbs
2 Tbsp onion soup powder
1 tsp sugar

Peel and cube the potatoes. Boil until soft, drain and mash together with the margarine, creamer, and salt and pepper to taste. Set aside.

Make up the beef stock and allow to cool.

Fry the onions in oil until glassy. Add the garlic, carrots and mince, and continue to fry, stirring all the time until the mince has cooked through. Stirring the mince while it cooks prevents it forming lumps.

Place the cooled beef stock, tomato paste, gravy powder, mixed herbs, onion soup and sugar into a bowl and mix well. Add this mixture to the mince and bring it to the boil, stirring continuously.

Reduce the heat, leave to simmer for a few minutes then remove from the stove.

Place the mince into an ovenproof dish and spread the mashed potato on top. If you want to be a little more creative, put the mash into a piping bag and pipe diagonal and horizontal lines over the top of the mince. As I always say, 'It's presentation, presentation, presentation!'.

Bake at 180 °C for 30–40 minutes until golden brown.

SERVES 4–6

Italian
BEEF SAUCE

THIS IS SUCH A VERSATILE SAUCE AND FOR THE SAME EFFORT IT'S WORTH DOUBLING UP ON THIS RECIPE AND FREEZING IT IN SMALLER PORTIONS. THEY TAKE A MINUTE OR TWO TO DEFROST IN THE MICROWAVE!

1 kg minced meat

oil for frying

2 medium onions, finely grated

1 carrot, finely grated

1 heaped tsp crushed garlic

½ cup red wine (optional)

1 x 410 g tin whole peeled tomatoes, chopped

2 cups beef stock (2 beef stock cubes to 2 cups boiling water)

3 Tbsp finely chopped fresh basil leaves

½ cup sun-dried tomato sauce

1 x 115 g tin tomato paste

1 tsp brown sugar

¾ cup cold water mixed with 1 Tbsp cornflour

1 tsp dried Italian herbs

½ tsp salt

little crushed black pepper

Fry the mince in a little oil, stirring continuously until golden brown. If you don't stir it while it's cooking, it may go rather 'clumpy and lumpy'. Once it's nicely browned, add the onions, carrot and garlic and continue to cook on medium to high heat until the onions are translucent. If you're using wine, add it now and leave it to simmer for a few minutes. Add the tinned tomatoes, beef stock and basil, reduce the heat and simmer, covered, on low for about 10 minutes.

Add the rest of the ingredients and simmer for a further 8–10 minutes, stirring every now and then. I find that the water and cornflour seem to bring everything together! Serve on spaghetti or your favourite pasta.

Note: Here are just a few ideas for using this sauce – Spaghetti Bolognaise, Bolognaise Twisters (page 186) or as a topping for cheeseless pizza bases. Use this mince as the base and add to it whatever you have a mouth for – try mushrooms, peppers, polony, pineapple or avocado. I'm sure you can think of a few too!

SERVES 4–6

whole
MEAL IN ONE

IT HAD BEEN A LONG DAY OUT IN THE GAME RESERVE. EVERYBODY WAS COLD, TIRED AND STARVING. NOT EVEN A LION OR A RHINO TO TALK ABOUT. BY NOW OUR EYES WERE HEAVY AND THAT EARLY-MORNING CRISP VISION WAS OUT OF FOCUS. HOWEVER, THERE WAS ONE THING THAT WAS GOING TO MAKE THIS EXHAUSTING DAY WORTHWHILE. A PIPING HOT MEAL WAITING FOR US IN THE OVEN. AND TO THINK THAT NOT ONE POT WAS USED TO MAKE IT – NOW THAT'S GOOD PLANNING!

1 whole round white pumpkin
500 g minced meat
2 chicken stock cubes dissolved in 2 cups boiling water
1 200 g packet rapid cook Spanish rice mix
1 x 405 g tin cream-style sweetcorn
1 x 405 g tin mushrooms
1 x 410 g tin peas
1 x 200 g packet rapid cook wild rice
1 x 65 g tin tomato paste
1 tsp salt
¼ tsp pepper
1 roll heavy-duty aluminium foil
1 disposable aluminium roasting tray

Wash the pumpkin well, then slice the top off about 2 cm down and put aside to use as a lid. Scoop out the flesh and pips until you have a nice clean cavity to fill. Don't scrape away too much flesh as you need a nice strong wall that shouldn't collapse while cooking!

Place the mince in the bottom of the cavity. Pour the hot stock directly onto the mince and mix it well. It should loosen and look as though the mince is already cooking!

Add the Spanish rice with spices and mix lightly with a spoon. Add the sweetcorn, tinned mushrooms and peas with all their liquid.

Add the other packet of rice, tomato paste, salt and pepper. Mix with a wooden spoon, getting really deep down. The texture should be quite loose, with a layer of liquid appearing as you press it down with the back of a spoon. The rice will absorb most of the liquid.

Place the pumpkin lid back onto the pumpkin. Place two large sheets of foil widthwise and two lengthwise on the aluminium roasting tray.

Position the pumpkin in the middle, pull the sides up and close them over the lid by twisting them together.

Place in the oven at 140 °C for at least 6–8 hours. In fact, we left ours cooking an entire day once and it was still delicious as it had formed a sticky toffee coating around the pumpkin.

If you're nervous that you don't have enough liquid, rather add a little more and when you get home, unwrap it, take the lid off, turn up the heat and allow a little liquid to evaporate. However, pumpkin naturally has its own liquid, which it gives off while cooking.

SERVES 6–8

MAINS – BEEF

steakhouse BEEF BURGER PATTIES

MY HUSBAND ALWAYS SAYS THE BEST WAY TO MAKE A BEEF PATTY IS WITH THE LEAST FUSS. HE FEELS THE PATTY SHOULD TASTE OF BEEF AND NOTHING ELSE. IF YOU WANT TO ADD BASTING SAUCE OR A NICE MUSHROOM SAUCE, THAT'S ANOTHER STORY, BUT THE BURGER ITSELF SHOULD BE MORE BEEF THAN BUN!

1 kg minced meat
1 large onion, grated
1 tsp freshly crushed garlic
2 eggs
½ cup breadcrumbs (my husband says no crumbs, I say a little – go with me on this one!)
2 Tbsp chopped fresh parsley or 2 tsp dried parsley
1 cup water
1 heaped tsp salt and pepper

Combine all the ingredients and roll into 250 g balls. Work gently with mince as over mixing can make meatballs too heavy and firm. When you're ready to fry them, press them down a little to flatten slightly and fry in a lightly oiled frying pan. Fry on medium to high heat until brown then turn over and brown the other side.

If they are very thick and you are worried that they may not be cooked on the inside, fry them on the one side until nicely browned, turn them over and cover the pan with a lid. This will help them to cook in the middle. Beef/chicken patties should never be pressed while cooking as the juices escape, resulting in a dry patty. Turn them with an egg lifter.

Serve on buns as they come out of the pan because this is when they are at their best. Leaving them in the warming oven or reheating them could make them dry and hard!

They can be served with onion rings (fried if you prefer), fresh tomato slices, cucumber and/or lettuce, piled up as high as you like.

Notes: The basting and barbecue sauces are what really give most steakhouse burgers their unique taste. Try to keep the beef patty as simple as possible (as per the recipe above) and then use either your favourite barbecue sauce or try the Butcher's Baster No. 1 on page 16.

For something different, why not try a burger braai? Instead of serving steak, chops and wors, serve the patties, buns, sauces, pickles, onions, tomatoes and every kind of condiment the children can find. Let everybody create their own masterpieces. Serve in brown paper bags.

Tip: Never partially cook a beef patty to reheat later!

MAKES 6 LARGE PATTIES

smoking MINCE CIGARS

WHERE THE ONLY THING SMOKING IS YOUR DESIRE FOR MORE! MY ELDEST SON WAS A BAD EATER AND WHEN WE FOUND SOMETHING HE LIKED WE MADE IT BY THE TRUCKLOAD! TO THIS DAY MY NEPHEW FROM AMERICA STILL REMEMBERS THOSE CIGARS HE LIVED ON IN SOUTH AFRICA ON A VISIT 17 YEARS AGO!

1 large onion, finely grated
1 tsp crushed garlic
little oil for frying
500 g minced meat
1 tsp ground cumin
½ tsp turmeric
2 tsp dried parsley
⅓ cup tomato sauce
salt and pepper
1 x 500 g box phyllo pastry

Fry the onion and garlic in a little oil until golden brown. Add the mince and mix well while you're cooking to keep it lump free.

Add the rest of the ingredients, except the pastry, and continue to mix. When cooked through, remove from the heat and leave to cool.

Take a sheet of phyllo pastry and cut it in half. Place 2 heaped tablespoons of the mince mixture in the top third of the pastry sheet. Spread it widthwise about 12 cm.

Fold in the sides and roll it up tightly so that it resembles a long thin cigar or a skinny version of a spring roll.

Spray with olive oil spray or paint with oil.

Bake in a preheated oven at 180 °C for approximately 10 minutes or until golden brown.

Serve with a sweet chilli sauce.

MAKES ±20

'PAP AND WORS' KEBABS
with tomato and onion dipping sauce

THIS IS A SIMPLE TWIST ON TRADITIONAL 'PAP AND WORS', THE NOVELTY BEING THAT THE GLAZED BOEREWORS AND MEALIE 'PAP' ARE ALL ON A STICK.

1 kg boerewors
12 wooden kebab sticks

FOR THE MEALIE 'PAP' BALLS
3 cups boiling water
1 tsp salt
1½ cups mealie meal, sifted
1 x 420 g tin cream-style sweetcorn

FOR THE DIPPING SAUCE
1 x 410 g tin braai relish
1 Tbsp apricot jam
1 Tbsp cornflour dissolved in ¾ cup cold water

FOR THE GLAZE
½ cup sweet chilli sauce
½ cup chutney (mild)

MEALIE 'PAP' BALLS:
Pour the water and salt into a medium-sized pot and bring to the boil. Slowly add the mealie meal, stirring continuously (preferably with a wooden spoon) until it forms a firmer consistency. Once all the mealie meal is well combined, add the sweetcorn and mix well.

Reduce the heat to low and simmer, covered, for 15–20 minutes. Remove from the pot and leave it to cool in a bowl.

BOEREWORS:
Soak the kebab sticks in water (this prevents them from burning when braaiing). While the mealie meal is cooking, place the boerewors into the microwave and cook for about 8–10 minutes on high (cover with paper towel). Leave the wors to cool, then cut into 3–4 cm pieces. (The boerewors must be cooked beforehand so that it doesn't fall apart when threaded onto the sticks.)

DIPPING SAUCE:
Make up the dipping sauce now and reheat it later when needed. Combine the braai relish, apricot jam and dissolved cornflour in a pot, bring to the boil, turn down the heat and allow it to simmer for a minute or two, stirring continuously.

When the mealie 'pap' has cooled, roll spoonfuls into small balls (smaller than golf balls). Thread pieces of wors and mealie 'pap' balls all the way along a kebab stick (press the balls firmly around the stick), leaving approximately 5 cm at the bottom for holding.

Paint the whole kebab (the meat and 'pap' balls) with the sweet chilli sauce and chutney glaze. Braai the kebabs until golden brown. Remember that they are already cooked, so all you need to do is brown them, heat them through and serve with dipping sauce.

MAKES ±12

110

Lamb and Veal

'di-luscious'
LAMB

THIS IS DEDICATED TO MY FRIEND DIANNE WHO ONLY ASKS FOR 'ANOREXIC' LAMB EVERY TIME SHE ORDERS IT. THERE IS NOTHING TO BEAT THE WONDERFUL TASTE OF LAMB THAT HAS BEEN MARINATED WITH ZESTY LEMONS, GARLIC AND FRESH HERBS, AND THEN ROASTED TO CRISP PERFECTION.

2.5–3 kg shoulder of lamb

FOR THE MARINADE
¼ cup olive oil
1 large onion, finely grated
1 tsp crushed garlic
1 Tbsp brown sugar
½ cup lemon juice
2 Tbsp chopped fresh parsley or
1 tsp dried parsley
6 long sprigs fresh rosemary or
1 Tbsp dried rosemary
1 Tbsp chopped fresh mint
1 tsp ground black pepper
sprinkling of salt

Combine the marinade ingredients and pour over the lamb. Make sure you get into all the nooks and crannies. Cover the meat and leave to marinate overnight.

Roast, covered, at 180 °C for 70 minutes. Remove the lid and roast for a further 60 minutes, turning the meat over and basting every now and then until it becomes golden brown and crispy.

When brown, reduce the heat to 160 °C and continue roasting for a further 30–45 minutes. Cover it again if you feel it's dark enough.

If the roast is bigger than 2.5 kg it will have to be cooked longer.

Note: If you have space in your roasting pan, add butternut chunks and halved baby potatoes. Spray them with olive oil and add them at the point where you uncover the roast after 70 minutes of roasting (no need to parboil them).

SERVES 8

apple mint-glazed
LAMB

WHETHER IT'S IN TEA, IN A SAUCE, DECORATING FRUIT OR ROASTING WITH LAMB, MINT HAS THE MOST WONDERFUL MEDICINAL QUALITIES. HOWEVER, IT DOES HAVE ITS SIDE EFFECTS, THOSE SIMILAR TO PARSLEY. ITS STRONG ADHESIVE QUALITY, ESPECIALLY WHEN IT COMES INTO CONTACT WITH TEETH, CAN TURN A ROMANTIC DINNER INTO A ROMANTIC DISASTER! SO, DON'T TRY THIS ONE OUT WHEN YOUR CHILD BRINGS HOME A PROSPECTIVE SHIDUCH (MARRIAGE POSSIBILITY) – THEY MAY JUST NOT HANG AROUND FOR DESSERT!

½ cup apple juice
½ cup apple sauce
½ cup mint jelly
2 Tbsp apple cider vinegar
1 Tbsp grainy mustard
2.5–3 kg shoulder of lamb
salt and ground black pepper
1 x 35 g packet fresh mint, roughly chopped
3 cloves garlic, thinly sliced

Preheat the oven to 180 °C. Combine the apple juice, apple sauce, mint jelly, vinegar and mustard. Pour the sauce over the lamb and sprinkle with a little salt and ground black pepper.

Place the mint leaves and garlic slices in between the bones, beneath the skin, on top, underneath and around the roast.

Place the meat in the oven and roast, meat side down, uncovered, for 1 hour, then turn the lamb over and roast for a further 30 minutes.

Turn it over one more time and continue roasting for a further 45 minutes, basting every now and then. This roast should turn a lovely rich, dark brown.

SERVES 8

lemon-kicked LAMB SHANKS

I HAD TO GET MY SISTER-IN-LAW TO HEAT UP HER LUKEWARM FEELINGS TOWARDS LAMB. YOU SEE, THERE WAS METHOD IN MY MADNESS – MY BROTHER LOVES LAMB AND, FOR HIS SAKE, I HAD TO CONVINCE HER. FINALLY, THIS WAS THE RECIPE THAT DID IT! WHAT WAS THE SECRET? MAYBE IT WAS THE LEMONS, MAYBE THE BRAAIING, WHO CARES! WHATEVER IT WAS, MY BROTHER NOW GETS LAMB!

8 lamb shanks (ask your butcher to nick them in two places)

FOR THE OVERNIGHT MARINADE
2 red or white onions, cut in half then sliced into rings
2 sticks lemon grass, sliced lengthwise down the middle, leaves separated and sliced into chunks
juice of 2 lemons
1½ tsp crushed garlic
sprinkling paprika
sprinkling lemon pepper
sprinkling mustard powder
5–6 sprigs fresh rosemary

Place half of the onions and lemon grass in the bottom of a marinating dish (preferably glass), and place the shanks on top.

Combine the lemon juice and garlic and pour over the shanks. Sprinkle the shanks with paprika, lemon pepper and mustard powder. Place the fresh rosemary on top of the meat followed by the other half of the onions and lemon grass.

Cover with clingfilm and refrigerate overnight. The next morning, turn the shanks over and again sprinkle with paprika, lemon pepper and mustard powder.

Place the shanks back in the fridge for a few hours.

If you're using a charcoal braai, prepare the braai an hour before you start cooking.

Once the flames have died down and the coals are glowing that lovely orange colour, place the naked shanks (discard the lemon grass, rosemary and onions) onto the grid. If you are using a braai with a lid, cover the shanks at this point for about 10–15 minutes, which helps to prevent the flames flaring up from the fat dripping from the shanks. However, keep turning them, and braai until golden brown on both sides.

The braaiing is just to give the shanks a healthy, barbecued look and taste. They still need to be roasted in the oven to cook through.

Place them in a roasting pan and roast, covered, in a preheated oven at 180 °C for 30 minutes.

Reduce the heat to 160 °C and continue roasting for a further 30–45 minutes. About 15 minutes before serving, uncover and roast just to crisp them up.

SERVES 12–14

DOUBLE-BREASTED MUSTARD SEED AND PEPPERCORN ENCRUSTED LAMB
with vegetable parcels

I CAN NEVER UNDERSTAND WHY LAMB BREASTS ARE SO HIGHLY UNDERRATED. THEY'RE TASTY, THEY COOK QUICKLY AND BECAUSE THEY ARE THIN, THE MARINADES PERMEATE RIGHT TO THE BONE!

3–4 breasts of lamb

FOR THE MARINADE
2 onions, sliced into rings
juice of 2 lemons
4 cloves garlic, crushed
1 tsp mustard powder
2 Tbsp onion soup powder
1 Tbsp mustard seeds or
2 tsp grainy mustard
¼ cup brown sugar
2 Tbsp mint jelly
4 sprigs rosemary (remove leaves from stalks)
couple of twists coarse salt
couple of twists coarsely ground pepper

FOR THE VEGETABLE PARCELS
500 g Mediterranean vegetables (available from Woolworths) or make up your own with brinjal, baby marrow, patty pans, peppers, baby onions and baby tomatoes
olive oil spray
1 tsp dried Italian herbs
±2 Tbsp balsamic vinegar
1 x 500 g box phyllo pastry

MARINADE:

Place the onion rings in the bottom of an ovenproof roasting dish. Place the lamb on top of the onions. Squeeze lemon juice over the lamb. Combine the remaining marinade ingredients and coat the lamb well. Leave to marinate overnight.

When you're ready to roast the breasts, drain off the excess marinade. Place, uncovered, in a preheated oven at 180 °C for 1–1½ hours. Turn the breasts over every now and then to ensure that they are evenly browned. If the ribs are cut up individually, they will probably need less roasting time than if they were left as a whole breast. However, they need to be roasted until dark and crispy.

SERVES 6–8

VEGETABLE PARCELS:

If you're not using the ready-cut and spiced vegetables, cube your vegetables and place on a roasting tray. Spray with a little olive oil spray and sprinkle with the herbs and balsamic vinegar. Place in the oven with the lamb and roast, uncovered, for 45–60 minutes.

Cut each sheet of phyllo pastry into quarters and place at least 2 squares into each lightly oiled muffin cup (use a 12-cup muffin tray for medium to large muffins). There will be quite a large pastry overlay. Keep the pastry you are not working with covered.

Place a heaped tablespoon of vegetables into each phyllo cup, draw up the sides of the pastry, twist it in the middle and spray with olive oil spray. Bake in the oven for 20 minutes before serving.

MAKES 12 (1–2 PER PERSON)

MOROCCAN-TEXTURED LAMB BREASTS
and pine nut couscous

MIXING DIFFERENT TEXTURES WHEN COOKING MAKES FOR EXCITING EATING! AND THAT'S WHAT THIS RECIPE IS ALL ABOUT. IT'S A COMBINATION OF HERBS AND SPICES AND CRUNCHY, COATED LAMB SERVED ON A FEATHER BED OF SOFT COUSCOUS, WITH EVERY MOUTHFUL A TEXTURE SENSATION.

3 breasts of lamb, cut into fingers (approximately 7 per breast)
½ tsp salt
1 tsp coarsely ground black pepper
1 onion, chopped
1 tsp freshly grated ginger
5 cloves garlic, crushed
2 Tbsp olive oil
1 Tbsp finely chopped fresh mint leaves
1 Tbsp finely chopped fresh coriander
1 tsp ground cumin
1 tsp paprika
1 Tbsp honey
1 x 410 g tin Mediterranean-style tomato and onions (All Gold™)
½ cup couscous (to be baked for topping)

FOR THE PINE NUT COUSCOUS
2 cups couscous
1 x 125 g packet pine nuts

Switch on the oven grill. Place the ribs in a roasting pan (meat facing you), sprinkle with salt and pepper, place under the grill and remove when brown and crispy. They will cook through properly later.

Fry the onion, ginger and garlic in the olive oil until soft. Add the mint leaves and coriander, and simmer for a few minutes, then add the cumin, paprika and honey, and mix well. Finally add the tin of tomato and onions.

Bring to the boil, reduce the heat and leave to simmer for a few minutes. Pour the sauce over the lamb and mix well so that all the ribs are well coated.

Roast, covered, in a preheated oven at 200 °C for 30 minutes. Remove the lid, turn the temperature down to 180 °C and continue roasting for 30–45 minutes, turning and basting continually.

While the lamb is roasting, place the couscous that needs to be baked onto a lightly oiled baking tray and bake until golden brown. Remove and set aside to cool, then make the pine nut couscous as per the recipe below.

Place the ribs on a bed of pine nuts and couscous, and sprinkle the baked, crunchy couscous over the top.

PINE NUT COUSCOUS:
Make the couscous according to the instructions on the packet. Bake the pine nuts in the oven or dry-fry them until golden brown. When the couscous is ready, fold in the pine nuts. The two textures really work well together.

SERVES 6–8

basted honey-mustard
SMOKED LAMB RIBS

SMOKED MEAT HAS A FLAVOUR ALL OF ITS OWN AND WHEN SMOKED RIBS ARE ENHANCED WITH A SAUCE OR GLAZE, THEY REALLY BECOME SOMETHING SPECIAL. IN FACT WHEN THESE RIBS ARE PUT ONTO OUR BRAAI, HALF OF THEM DON'T MAKE IT TO THE TABLE – THE BRAAI CHEFS AND THEIR ASSISTANTS SEEM TO FEEL THAT THERE HAS TO BE SOME KIND OF REWARD FOR SMOKE GETTING IN THEIR EYES!

3 smoked breasts of lamb

FOR THE BASTING SAUCE
1 Tbsp prepared
Hot English mustard
¼ cup honey
2 Tbsp ginger syrup
1 Tbsp apricot jam
¼ cup soy sauce
2 Tbsp lemon juice
¼ cup chutney

If you are going to roast the ribs rather than braai them, preheat the oven to 200 °C. Place all the ingredients for the basting sauce into a pot and heat through. As the sauce starts to boil, remove it from the heat. (Or, if you're in a hurry, use readily available sachets of honey-mustard basting sauces.)

Remove any visible fat from the ribs (a lot of the fat does cook out when they start cooking).

Paint the breasts with the sauce and bake, uncovered, in the oven until crispy. This normally takes 40–45 minutes. If cut up individually they will take less time, but that also depends on how crispy you like them.

Remember that the ribs are basically cooked, as they have already been cooked and smoked. They simply need to be heated through and crisped.

Lamb breasts are just as delicious basted and cooked on the braai.

Note: Smoked breasts of lamb have to be ordered a few days in advance, as they have to be cooked and smoked.

SERVES 2–3 PEOPLE PER RACK

mock OXTAIL

'WHY CAN'T WE GET KOSHER OXTAIL?' THIS MUST BE ONE OF THE MOST POPULAR QUESTIONS FACING KOSHER BUTCHERS. UNFORTUNATELY THE TAIL IS PROBABLY ONE OF THE MOST DIFFICULT PARTS OF THE ANIMAL TO DE-VEIN (FOR KOSHERING PURPOSES) AND DURING THIS PROCESS IT COULD END UP LOOKING A LITTLE WORSE FOR WEAR! MAYBE WHAT WE'RE REALLY MISSING IS THE UNIQUE FLAVOUR OF THIS SLOW-COOKED DISH AND THE WAY THE MEAT 'JUST FALLS OFF THE BONE'! HOPEFULLY THIS VERSION OF 'OXTAIL' WILL OFFER ALL THAT AND MORE!

1.5–2 kg neck of lamb
2 Tbsp gravy powder mixed with
½ cup flour
little oil for frying
1 cup red wine
2 Tbsp tomato paste
2 onions, roughly chopped
4 large carrots, sliced 1 cm thick
3 sticks celery, sliced 1 cm thick
2 tsp pressed or finely chopped garlic
1 tsp freshly grated ginger
1 Tbsp finely chopped fresh parsley or ¾ tsp dried parsley
1 Tbsp chopped fresh thyme or ¾ tsp dried thyme
1 cup home-made chicken stock or 1 chicken stock cube dissolved in 1 cup boiling water
1 cup beef stock (1 beef stock cube dissolved in 1 cup boiling water)
1 x 410 g tin small white beans (reserve the liquid)
2 bay leaves
salt and pepper

Preheat the oven to 180 °C. Roll the lamb in the gravy powder and flour mixture until all the pieces are well coated. Pour a little oil in a heavy-based saucepan or large frying pan and fry the meat for a few minutes just to brown it. The meat must not burn, as the vegetables and wine still have to be cooked in the same pan.

Remove the meat from the pan and place it in a medium-sized casserole or roasting dish.

Pour the wine into the frying pan or saucepan and bring to the boil. While the wine is simmering, add the tomato paste and keep stirring. Pour this over the meat.

Return the pan to the heat, add a little oil and fry the onions, carrots, celery, garlic, ginger, parsley and thyme for a few minutes. Remove the vegetables from the pan and place them on top of the meat in the casserole or roasting pan.

Add the chicken and beef stock to the meat and vegetables, and mix well. Add the tinned beans (with liquid) and place a bay leaf at either end of the dish. Grind a little salt and pepper over the meat.

Cover the casserole or roasting dish with a lid or aluminium foil, and cook in the oven for 1 hour. Reduce the heat to 160 °C, give it a gentle stir and continue to cook, covered, for a further 1–1½ hours or until tender. If you think the gravy is too watery, remove the lid or foil for the last 30 minutes to allow it to reduce and thicken.

Serve with mashed potatoes, peas and bread for dunking!

Note: Ask the butcher for whole necks cut into 3 cm thick slices – like thick rings.

SERVES 6–8

blushing
TOMATO BREDIE

FOR THOSE WITH A PASSION FOR VALENTINE RED TOMATOES, THIS SHOULD BRING A HINT OF PINK TO YOUR CHEEKS. BLUSH AWAY THOSE INHIBITIONS AND TICKLE HIS TASTE BUDS WITH THIS TOMATO TEMPTER.

2 kg neck of lamb or stewing lamb on the bone
½ cup flour mixed with 2 Tbsp onion soup powder
little oil for frying
8 large red tomatoes
1 tsp crushed garlic
1 x 410 g tin tomato, basil and garlic mix
1 Tbsp tomato paste
1½ cups cold water
½ cup tomato chutney
2 Tbsp tomato jam
juice of 1 freshly squeezed orange
1 tsp grated orange rind
1 tot sherry (optional)
1 heaped tsp brown sugar
1 tsp dried thyme or a few sprigs fresh thyme
salt and pepper

Roll the lamb in the flour and onion soup powder.

In a large, heavy-based pot brown the outside of the lamb in a little oil. Fry small batches at a time. When brown, remove from the pot and set aside.

While the meat is frying, prepare the tomatoes. Place them in a bowl of boiling water for a minute, then peel off the skins. Cut the tomatoes in half horizontally and scoop out the pips. If they don't all come out 'dis nisht geferelech', it's not that serious!

Chop the tomatoes into small pieces, then place with the rest of the ingredients into the same pot in which the lamb was fried.

Bring to the boil, stirring as you do to get all the bits of meat off the bottom. Return the lamb to the pot and give it a good stir, making sure the meat is well coated with the sauce.

Reduce the heat and leave it to simmer, covered, for 30–45 minutes on low. It should make its own liquid, but if you find the sauce a little too thick, add a little more water. It's better to have more water, which evaporates when the lid is removed, than too little and it burns. That burnt smell and taste can't be removed!

Continue to simmer on low for at least another hour until the meat is soft, stirring every now and then to prevent sticking. Switch off the stove and leave the lamb to sit for about 30 minutes, absorbing all the lovely flavours. When you're ready to eat, bring it to the boil, stirring gently as you heat it through.

Serve on a bed of parsley rice with green beans.

Note: Place 2 teaspoons of dried parsley into the water in which you are going to cook the rice. I normally use 2 cups of uncooked rice and follow the cooking instructions on the packet.

SERVES 8

LAMB CURRY
in a hurry

THIS IS QUITE A SPICY CURRY AND NOT SUITABLE FOR THE FAINT-HEARTED! HOWEVER, YOU CAN TONE IT DOWN BY USING A MILD OR MEDIUM CHAKALAKA. OR TAKE A CHANCE, AND KEEP A SPARE SERVIETTE HANDY TO MOP YOUR BROW!

1.5 kg sliced neck of lamb or
1.5 kg sliced stewing lamb
½ cup flour
little oil for frying
1 tsp crushed garlic
1 x 35 g packet fresh coriander,
finely chopped
⅓ cup peri-peri sauce (strength
depends on your chilli level
tolerance!)
1 x 200 ml sachet Ina Paarman™
curried tikka sauce (kosher)
2 sachets water (fill the tikka
sauce sachet)
1 x 410 g tin hot chakalaka (if you
prefer it a little milder, use mild)
1 tin water
1 Tbsp brown sugar
salt and pepper
½ cup coconut milk (optional)

Coat the lamb lightly in flour. In a large pot brown the lamb in a little oil.

Pour off the excess oil before adding the remaining ingredients, except the coconut milk, and stir well.

Bring the meat to the boil, then reduce the heat and leave it to simmer, covered, on low heat. Stir every so often to prevent burning at the bottom of the pot.

After 1–1½ hours the meat should be soft. If not, leave it to carry on cooking until soft, adding more water if necessary.

Once the meat is soft, switch off the heat and leave the curry to sit quietly 'with its arms folded' until needed!

Just before serving, reheat and add the coconut milk or ½ cup water if it needs more liquid.

Serve with rice.

Note: If you're in a real hurry, use chicken pieces. They cook in half the time! And if you don't even have time for that, use chicken schnitzel!

SERVES 6

CRUMBED VEAL/LAMB
with creamed broccoli sauce

NEED TO WHIP UP SOMETHING THAT'S TIME EASING AND APPETITE PLEASING? THEN LOOK NO FURTHER, 'CAUSE IT'S CHOPS YOU'LL BE SEIZING!

8 chops, marinated for no more than 1 hour in the juice of 2 lemons

3 well-beaten eggs

oil for frying

FOR THE CRUMB MIXTURE

1½ cups breadcrumbs or cornflake crumbs

½ cup brown or nutty wheat flour

½ tsp garlic salt

1 tsp paprika

1 tsp lemon pepper seasoning

2 Tbsp onion soup powder

½ tsp dried origanum

1 tsp mustard powder

salt and pepper

FOR THE BROCCOLI SAUCE

250–300 g packet fresh or frozen broccoli

1 onion, finely chopped

2 Tbsp non-dairy margarine

1 heaped Tbsp flour

1 level Tbsp chicken stock powder

1 tsp mustard powder

1 cup non-dairy creamer

1 cup water

salt and pepper

Preheat the oven to 180 °C. Remove the lamb chops from the lemon juice and pat dry with paper towel.

Dip the chops into the beaten egg and then into the crumb mixture. Place the chops on a lightly floured board until ready to fry.

Fry the chops in oil until golden brown on the outside. Don't be concerned if they are not cooked right through, as they are still placed into the oven on a baking tray for further cooking (if you see blood seeping through near the bone while frying, they are not ready).

Place the chops in the oven for about 10 minutes or until they are cooked through.

CRUMB MIXTURE:

Mix all the ingredients together and place in a flat dish.

CREAMED BROCCOLI SAUCE:

Clean the fresh broccoli well, or simply cut off the florets, as they are difficult to check for insects, and use the stems only. Steam until soft. Defrost the frozen broccoli.

Fry the chopped onion in the margarine and, when glassy, remove from the heat. Add the flour, stock powder and mustard to the onions, and mix well so that all the onions are well coated.

While the onions are still off the heat, add the non-dairy creamer and water, and mix well. Put the onion mixture back onto the heat and bring to the boil, stirring continuously. As it starts to bubble, add the broccoli, gently stirring as you do so. Add salt and pepper to taste. Turn the heat down and allow it to simmer, covered, for about 5 minutes. Switch off the stove and blend the sauce until smooth. Reheat when ready to serve.

SERVES 4–6

MAINS – LAMB AND VEAL

Jeff's
STUFFED BREAST OF VEAL

WHAT A PLEASURE IT IS TO FEED MY COUSIN JEFF. WHETHER IT'S A PIECE OF KRAKELWURST WITH A WHISKY OR A COCKTAIL DIPPED IN MUSTARD, TO HIM IT'S ALL GOOD! BUT THE ONE THING THAT REALLY TIPS THE SCALES IN MY FAVOUR IS STUFFED BREAST OF VEAL!

1 breast of veal (ask your butcher to cut a pocket in the veal)

1 x 500 g packet kishke stuffing (or home-made stuffing)

1 Tbsp oil

2 onions, cut into rings

300 g carrots, pre-cut julienne style

4 sticks celery, thinly sliced

1 x 500 g punnet peeled and chopped butternut or pumpkin

4 potatoes, cut in half

FOR THE SPICE RUB

½ tsp paprika

1 tsp ground black pepper

½ tsp garlic salt

1 tsp mustard powder

½ tsp onion salt

FOR THE HOME-MADE STUFFING

2 onions, chopped

½ cup oil

1 chicken stock cube dissolved in ¾ cup boiling water

1½–2 cups flour, sifted

1½ tsp baking powder

salt and pepper

Preheat the oven to 190 °C. Fill the veal pocket with the kishke (or home-made) stuffing and pack it in well.

Pour the oil over the veal and rub it over the roast with your hands. Pour the spice rub into your oiled hands and rub over the veal.

Place the onions, carrots and celery into a large roasting pan (lightly oiled on the bottom). Place the veal, meat side down, bones facing upwards, on top of the vegetables. Place the butternut and potatoes around the meat. Sprinkle a little more oil over the vegetables or spray with olive oil.

Roast, uncovered, for 45 minutes. Reduce the temperature to 180 °C, turn the roast over and cover it with aluminium foil. Roast for another hour.

Remove the foil, reduce the heat to 170 °C and roast for a further 45–60 minutes until the meat and vegetables are golden brown.

HOME-MADE STUFFING:
Fry the onions in the oil until brown. Add the chicken stock and stir, getting all the bits of onion off the base of the pan. Remove from the heat.

Add the flour, baking powder, and salt and pepper to taste. Mix well together. This should be quite a soft stuffing but firm enough to pack into the veal.

SERVES 6–8

MAINS – LAMB AND VEAL

STUFFED BREAST OF MEDITERRANEAN VEAL
with roasted pumpkin and spiced sunflower seeds

IF YOU'RE LIKE MY HUSBAND AND DON'T LIKE MEAT STUFFED, MAKE UP THE STUFFING RECIPE AND SERVE IT AS AN ACCOMPANIMENT TO THE VEAL. YOU CAN ALSO THROW A COUPLE OF OLIVES AROUND THE MEAT, BUT, IF YOU'RE LIKE ME AND DON'T LIKE OLIVES, JUST LEAVE THEM OUT! NOW, THAT'S JUST TWO FUSSY EATERS. IMAGINE TRYING TO SATISFY SIX DURING THE WEEK AND NINETEEN EVERY FRIDAY NIGHT! BUT THAT'S WHAT FAMILY'S ALL ABOUT, AND WITHOUT THEIR SOMETIMES RATHER HARSH CRITICISM, THIS BOOK WOULD NEVER HAVE HAPPENED!

1 large breast of veal (let your butcher cut a pocket for stuffing)

FOR THE STUFFING
2 cups couscous, cooked according to the instructions on the box
1 x 410 g tin Mediterranean ratatouille mix
½ tsp crushed garlic
1 x 405 g tin mushrooms, drained
salt and pepper

FOR THE MEAT SPICE
juice of 1 lemon
½ tsp garlic salt
½ tsp ground cumin
½ tsp ground ginger
¼ tsp ground cinnamon
2 Tbsp onion soup powder

FOR THE ROASTED PUMPKIN AND SPICED SUNFLOWER SEEDS
½ cup sunflower seeds
2 Tbsp peri-peri sauce (medium)
1 kg peeled and cubed pumpkin
little oil for roasting
3 Tbsp soft brown treacle sugar
1 tsp ground cinnamon

Preheat the oven to 180 °C. Combine the ready-made couscous, ratatouille mix, garlic, mushrooms, and salt and pepper to taste. Stuff the pocket of the veal with this mixture.

Pour the juice of the lemon over the meaty part of the veal. Combine the meat spices together and rub over the entire piece of meat.

Roast, covered, in the oven for 1 hour. If you're not stuffing the veal, roast it, covered, for 45 minutes. Remove the cover and continue roasting for another hour, basting every now and then, and leaving the roast to turn brown and become crisp.

During the final hour of roasting, start roasting the pumpkin and sunflower seeds.

ROASTED PUMPKIN AND SPICED SUNFLOWER SEEDS:
Place the sunflower seeds into a small bowl. Add the peri-peri sauce and mix well, ensuring that the seeds are lightly coated.

Bake on a baking tray in a preheated oven at 180 °C, until they become golden brown and crispy. Remove and allow to cool.

Place the pumpkin into a roasting dish, drizzle with a little oil and sprinkle with the treacle sugar and cinnamon.

Bake, uncovered, for 45 minutes or until golden brown. It's always difficult to give a definite baking time because sizes vary and larger pieces of pumpkin take longer.

Remove from the oven, place in a serving dish and sprinkle with the spicy sunflower seeds.

SERVES 6

Poultry

TURKEY
– in-laws and outlaws get stuffed!

WHEN IT COMES TO TURKEYS, I AM REMINDED OF MY MOTHER-IN-LAW AND HER FAMOUS YOMTOV TURKEY! NOBODY CAN ROAST A TURKEY TO PERFECTION LIKE HER – EVEN MY MOTHER AGREES! BUT THEN NOBODY MAKES STUFFING QUITE LIKE MY MOTHER, SO I'M INCLUDING HER STUFFING RECIPE THAT JUST HAPPENS TO COME SURROUNDED BY MY MOTHER-IN-LAW'S ROASTED TURKEY!

5–6 kg turkey
½ cup oil
2 tsp salt
1 tsp pepper
1½ tsp barbecue spice
½ tsp ground ginger
1 tsp garlic salt
1½ tsp paprika
1 onion, peeled (optional)

FOR THE STUFFING (ADD 1 HOUR TO THE ROASTING TIME WHEN USING STUFFING)
1 loaf white bread, crusts removed
250 g beef pastrami
2 onions, chopped
±15 fresh sage leaves, finely chopped or 1 tsp dried sage
2 sticks celery, finely chopped
little oil for frying
1 cup chicken stock (if you've made for Yomtov) or 1 chicken stock cube dissolved in ¾ cup boiling water

Cover the entire turkey with the oil. Combine the spices and rub them all over the turkey. You've heard the saying 'getting under my skin'? So really rub it in everywhere. Place an onion into the cavity unless you're stuffing it.

'Never mind what anybody tells you, you roast that turkey, uncovered, for at least 3½ hours in the oven at 180 °C, and if it looks like it's getting too dark, turn the oven down a bit, but keep on roasting!' said my mother-in-law.

'If I stuff the turkey, how much longer should I roast it?' I asked her. 'I don't know, that's why I don't stuff mine!' she replied.

STUFFING:

Cut the bread into cubes. Place the cubes into a large bowl. Chop the pastrami into very small pieces and add it to the bread cubes.

Fry the onions, sage and celery in a little oil until soft. Place the onion and celery mixture into the same bowl as the pastrami and bread.

Pour the stock over the bread to be absorbed as you mash the bread with a fork. Don't add all the stock at once, as you may not need it all.

The bread should be moist but not so soggy that it falls apart when you lift it, but you shouldn't be able to see any bits of dry bread!

Press the stuffing into the turkey cavity and place it in the oven to roast for about 4 hours.

Tip: Now here's the tip that a friend once gave my mother-in-law: 30 minutes before taking the turkey out of the oven, squeeze the juice of two oranges over it and put it back in to roast.

SERVES 10–12

Thanksgiving
PECAN PUMPKIN PASTA

BEING IN AMERICA VISITING FAMILY OVER THANKSGIVING ONE YEAR WAS A NEW EXPERIENCE. THIS WAS LIKE NO OTHER HOLIDAY! TRADITIONALLY, AS WE SO OFTEN SEE ON THE AMERICAN SITCOMS, THE TURKEY TAKES CENTRE STAGE WITH ITS SUPPORTING STARS, THE PUMPKIN AND PECAN NUT PIES. HOWEVER, THIS PERFORMANCE OF THANKSGIVING HAD ALL THE STARS, BUT IN DIFFERENT ROLES! IT WAS TURKEY AND PUMPKIN PASTA WITH PECANS AS THE CHORUS!

250 g peeled and cubed (1 cm cubes) butternut (we used the frozen variety)
olive oil spray
½ tsp cinnamon mixed with
1 Tbsp brown sugar
500 g thinly sliced turkey schnitzel
2 Tbsp chicken stock powder
1 chicken stock cube dissolved in
2½ cups boiling water
1 x 405 g tin mushrooms
1 heaped Tbsp cornflour
1½ cups soya milk
salt and pepper
500 g fettuccine pasta
salted pecan nuts, crushed

Preheat the oven to 180 °C. Place the butternut in a roasting pan, spray with a little olive oil and sprinkle with cinnamon and brown sugar. Place in the oven and bake for 30 minutes until golden brown.

Slice the turkey into thin, bite-size strips. Lightly sprinkle with chicken stock powder and fry it in small batches in a lightly oiled pan. Fry the turkey until golden on both sides. Remove from the pan and set aside. Repeat this process until all the turkey has been cooked.

Remove the pan from the heat and add the chicken stock.

Drain the liquid off the tinned mushrooms and dissolve the cornflour in this liquid. Add the soya milk to the cornflour mixture and mix well. Add to the chicken stock mixture and return to the heat. Bring to the boil, stirring continuously with a whisk.

When it starts to thicken, add the turkey and mushrooms. Give it a good stir, remove it from the heat and set aside. Add salt and pepper to taste.

By now the pumpkin should be ready. Remove it from the oven and set aside.

When you are ready to serve the meal, cook the pasta according to the instructions on the packet.

Heat the turkey and mushroom sauce, stirring as you do so. Lastly, add the pumpkin, mixing it carefully so as not to mash it up too much.

As soon as the pasta is ready, pour the turkey, mushroom and pumpkin mixture over the pasta and sprinkle with pecan nuts.

SERVES 6–8

134

fresh garden
HERBED CHICKEN

I WAS TIRED OF NEVER HAVING FRESH HERBS WHEN I NEEDED THEM, SO THE ONLY WAY OUT WAS TO START GROWING MY OWN. WHEREVER YOU LOOKED YOU SAW HERBS POKING THEIR LITTLE HEADS OUT REMINDING ME TO USE THEM. SO BEFORE THEY BECAME TOO OVERGROWN, I TRIMMED THEM BACK AND USED THEM IN THIS CHICKEN DISH.

½ cup oil

6 cloves garlic, crushed

juice of 2 lemons

2 tsp paprika

1 Tbsp peri-peri sauce

1 handful fresh sage leaves (about 10), finely chopped

1 handful fresh flat-leaf parsley, finely chopped

1 spatchcock chicken

8 sprigs rosemary

salt and pepper

Preheat the oven to 180 °C. Place the oil, garlic, lemon juice, paprika, peri-peri sauce, chopped sage and parsley into a bowl and mix. Pour half of the mixture over the skin of the chicken and rub into all the nooks and crannies.

Place the rosemary sprigs in the bottom of a roasting pan, so that they will lie beneath the chicken.

Carefully place the chicken, skin side down, on top of the rosemary sprigs (the cavity will be facing you) and place the remaining herb sauce inside and around the cavity.

Roast for 45 minutes, uncovered, then turn the chicken over, and roast, still uncovered, for a further 45 minutes or until golden brown. Baste every now and then with its own juices.

SERVES 4–6

CURRIED CHICKEN RING
with fried bananas

WHENEVER I MAKE CURRY THERE'S ALWAYS SOMETHING I FORGET TO SERVE WITH IT. WHETHER IT'S THE BANANAS, CHUTNEY, OR TOMATO AND ONION SAMBAL, I ALWAYS FORGET ONE. INEVITABLY, IT'S THE ONE SOMEBODY WILL ASK FOR. SO I DEVELOPED A METHOD TO REMIND ME NOT TO LEAVE ANYBODY'S FAVOURITE SAMBAL OUT OF THE PICTURE.

1 kg chicken (ask your butcher to cut it into small pieces, shuwarma style)
½ tsp turmeric
½ tsp paprika
½ tsp ground cumin
½ tsp garlic salt
½ tsp ground coriander
pinch ground cloves
½ tsp ground ginger
1 tsp curry powder
2 cups basmati rice
½ cup desiccated coconut
2 tomatoes
1 small onion
2 Tbsp brown vinegar
4 bananas, cut into 1 cm slices and sprinkled with ½ tsp ground cinnamon, 2 Tbsp brown sugar and 2 Tbsp lemon juice
1 large onion, chopped
little oil for frying
3 Tbsp chutney (mild or hot)
1 Tbsp cornflour dissolved in 1 cup cold water
½ cup chutney (mild or hot)
chopped fresh coriander for garnishing

Place all the spices into a bowl and mix well. Sprinkle these spices over the chicken mixing it well. Cover and leave the chicken to absorb all the flavours while you prepare the rest of the dish.

Cook the rice according to the instructions on the box. Toast the coconut under the grill until golden brown. Remove and set aside.

Chop the tomatoes and 1 small onion, and mix together. Sprinkle with a little vinegar, cover and refrigerate until needed.

Fry the bananas in a non-stick pan until soft but not mushy (they should still retain their shape and have a lovely golden glaze from the sugar). Leave them in the pan until you're ready to decorate the chicken dish – they can be reheated or served at room temperature.

Fry the chopped onion in a little oil until golden brown. When cooked, remove from the pan and set aside. Add a little more oil to the pan and fry small batches of chicken until golden brown. Return all the chicken to the pan, add the fried onion, 3 Tbsp chutney and the cornflour mixture. Bring to the boil, reduce the heat, cover and allow to simmer for about 20 minutes. Switch off the heat and leave the chicken to rest and absorb the curry flavour.

In the meantime the rice should be ready. Reheat it if it has cooled. Pack the rice into a ring mould. Reheat the chicken, and turn the rice out onto the centre of a large, round serving platter.

Pour the chicken into the centre of the rice ring. Place spoonfuls of bananas around the outer edge of the platter, alternating with spoonfuls of chutney and chopped tomato and onion. Decorate the curry with chopped coriander and finally sprinkle the crisp coconut over the entire dish as if you were feeding chickens in a farmyard (with smaller hand movements of course!).

SERVES 4–5

chunky Mexican
SWEET CHILLI CHICKEN

THIS IS A QUICK AND EASY MEXICAN DISH THAT HAS A UNIQUE SPICY AND YET SWEET FLAVOUR, GIVING IT THAT HINT OF 'ARRIBA' AND KICK OF JORGE CAMPOS!

2 onions, roughly chopped
oil for frying
1 heaped tsp brown treacle sugar
6–8 pieces of your favourite
skinless chicken portions,
seasoned with salt and pepper
¼ cup sweet chilli sauce
1 x 410 g tin Mexican tomato
and onion mix
1 x 405 g cream style sweetcorn
½ can cold water
1 cup frozen corn (defrosted)
500 g Heinz® Potato Bites

Preheat the oven to 180 °C. In a large, heavy-based pot, fry the onions in a little oil. As the onions start to brown, add the treacle sugar, then place into a medium-sized ovenproof dish or roasting pan.

In the same pot used to fry the onions, fry the chicken pieces on both sides until brown and place side by side on top of the onions in the ovenproof dish. Don't be concerned if they're not cooked through as they still have to bake in the oven.

Combine the sweet chilli sauce and Mexican mix and pour over the chicken.

Mix together the sweetcorn, water and frozen corn, and pour in a layer on top of the Mexican mix.

Finally cover the corn with a tightly packed layer of potato bites.

Bake, covered, in the oven for 35 minutes. Remove the cover and cook for a further 35–45 minutes until the potatoes are golden brown. If using chicken schnitzels, or any deboned chicken, reduce the baking to 25 minutes, covered, and 20–30 minutes, uncovered, or until the potato bites are golden brown.

SERVES 6

CHILLI-CHILLI CHICKEN
and corncob muffins

ALTHOUGH THE DOUBLE-CHILLI SAUCE GIVES THE CHICKEN AN INTERESTING BITE, IT'S SOMEHOW SOOTHED BY THE MILD SWEETNESS OF THE CORNCOB MUFFINS. I THINK IT'S IMPORTANT WHEN COOKING SOMETHING SPICY TO COMPLEMENT IT WITH SOMETHING SOOTHING. FOOD SHOULDN'T ATTACK YOUR SENSE OF TASTE AND SMELL WITH STRONG HERBS AND SPICES, BUT RATHER RE-AWAKEN YOUR TASTE BUDS TO SOMETHING DIFFERENT.

6 thick chicken schnitzels
½ cup flour
little peri-peri oil for frying
½ cup orange juice
¼ cup sweet chilli sauce
1 Tbsp chilli sauce (strength depends on you!)
1 Tbsp cornflour dissolved in ½ cup cold water
1 Tbsp chicken stock powder
salt and pepper

FOR THE CORNCOB MUFFINS
2 Tbsp non-dairy margarine
2 Tbsp sugar
2 eggs
½ tsp salt
¾ cup flour
½ cup mealie meal
1 Tbsp onion soup powder
¼ cup water
1½ tsp baking powder
¼ tsp black pepper
1 x 410 g tin cream-style sweetcorn
½ cup frozen corn

Preheat the oven to 180 °C. Dust the schnitzels with the flour and fry in a little peri-peri oil until brown. Avoid burning the bottom of the frying pan, as you need to fry the other ingredients in the same pan. Remove the chicken and place in an ovenproof dish.

Combine the rest of the ingredients and place in the pan. Bring to the boil and, as the sauce starts to thicken slightly, remove it from the heat. Stir well and pour over the chicken, making sure each piece is well glazed.

Bake in the oven, uncovered, for 20 minutes. Turn over and bake until golden brown on the other side.

CORNCOB MUFFINS:
Preheat the oven to 180 °C. Cream the margarine, sugar, eggs and salt until light and fluffy. Add the flour, mealie meal, onion soup powder, water, baking powder and pepper, and blend until smooth. Fold in the tinned sweetcorn and frozen corn.

Grease and flour a 12-cup muffin tin. Half fill each muffin cup and bake for 35–40 minutes.

Remove the muffins from the tin, cut in half and place a chicken schnitzel in each. I serve mine with a 'chillinaise' sauce, which is made up of 2 Tbsp sweet chilli sauce and ½ cup mayonnaise.

MAKES 6 LARGE OR 12 SMALL MUFFINS (CUT SCHNITZELS IN HALF IF MAKING 12 MUFFINS)

crispy CHICKEN PUFFS

THESE CAN EITHER BE SERVED AS COCKTAILS, SOMETHING TO MUNCH ON WHILE STUDYING OR TO YOUR NEPHEW WHO WON'T EAT CHICKEN UNLESS IT'S HIS AUNTIE'S CHICKEN PUFFS! I SUPPOSE THIS IS WHAT THEY MEAN BY A 'WIN-WIN' SITUATION – IT FEEDS THE YOUNG, THE RESTLESS AND THE RETIRED!

6 thick chicken schnitzels
barbecue spice
salt
½ cup self-raising flour
½ cup cornflour
1 cup cold water
750 ml–1 litre oil
1 cup sweet-and-sour sauce
(available at most supermarkets)

Cut each schnitzel in half lengthwise and then in half again or in thirds, making four or six pieces (depending on the size of the schnitzel). Sprinkle with barbecue spice and salt, and set aside.

Sift the flour and cornflour into a bowl and make a well in the middle. Pour the water into the well and whisk or mix with a hand blender until a smooth batter is formed. Leave it to rest for a few minutes.

Heat the oil in a deep frying pan. Place the chicken pieces in the batter and ensure that they are well coated.

Gently immerse the chicken pieces, one by one, into the hot oil. Don't fry more than four or five at once as this will reduce the temperature of the oil and the chicken won't become crisp and get that lovely, all-over golden tan!

As they turn brown, remove them and leave them to drain on brown paper.

Place them in a warm oven at 100–120 °C to keep warm while the others are cooking (don't cover them, as they will lose their crispness and become soggy).

Place toothpicks in the centre of each chicken puff and serve on a platter around a small bowl of sweet-and-sour dipping sauce. Most supermarkets carry a range of kosher sweet-and-sour sauces.

SERVES 6

protein-packed POULET

ACCORDING TO OUR PAEDIATRICIAN, COAXING MY BABIES INTO EATING THEIR PURÉED VEGETABLES WOULD BE EASY. 'JUST LACE IT WITH PEANUT BUTTER,' HE SAID. SO THANKS DR HEITNER, A PROTEIN-PACKED PEANUT BUTTER SANDWICH IS STILL THEIR FAVOURITE! THEY EVEN SWAP THEIR COLD MEAT BAGELS FOR THEM AT SCHOOL!

1 large onion, chopped
3 cloves garlic, crushed
oil for frying
8 chicken schnitzels, cut lengthwise into 3 or 4 pieces
1 chicken stock cube dissolved in 1 cup boiling water
3 Tbsp soy sauce
1 Tbsp brown sugar
1 heaped Tbsp peanut butter
1 Tbsp sweet chilli sauce
2 tsp peri-peri sauce
1 heaped Tbsp cornflour, dissolved in ¾ cup cold water
½ cup sesame seeds
handful roughly chopped coriander to garnish (optional)

Use a large frying pan, wok or pot as everything is cooked in one pot.

Fry the onion and garlic in a little oil. When the onion starts to brown, remove it from the pan and place in a glass or plastic bowl large enough to hold the chicken once it has been cooked.

Add a little more oil to the pan and fry the chicken pieces (about five or six at a time) until golden brown, and place in the same dish as the onions.

To the same pan add the chicken stock, soy sauce, brown sugar, peanut butter, sweet chilli sauce, peri-peri sauce and dissolved cornflour mixture. Bring to the boil until the sauce thickens slightly, then reduce the heat.

Place the chicken and onions back into the pan and simmer for about 15 minutes, stirring gently.

Serve on a bed of jasmine rice and sprinkle with the sesame seeds and chopped coriander.

SERVES 8

FETTUCCINE
à la king

THE NAME SAYS IT ALL. A CREAMY, NON-DAIRY ALFREDO SAUCE WITH THE DELICIOUS TASTE OF CHICKEN À LA KING!

1 red pepper
1 green pepper
1 yellow pepper
oil for frying
400 g sliced mushrooms
1 heaped tsp crushed garlic
1 hot red chilli, finely chopped (optional)
1 Tbsp finely chopped fresh parsley or 1 tsp dried parsley
¼ cup flour
1 tsp mustard powder
1 Tbsp chicken stock powder
salt and pepper
750 g chicken, cut shuwarma style
3 cups cold water
2 heaped Tbsp cornflour
1 cup non-dairy creamer or Orley Whip™
ground black pepper
500 g fettuccine pasta
fresh flat-leaf parsley to garnish

Wash and remove the seeds from the peppers, slice into thin strips and fry in a deep frying pan in a little oil. Add the mushrooms and, when most of the liquid has evaporated, add the garlic, chilli and parsley. Cook for a few more minutes, then set aside in a dish.

Combine the flour, mustard powder, chicken stock powder, and salt and pepper to taste, and sift over the chicken pieces. Roll and coat the chicken in the flour and spice mixture.

Add a little oil to the same frying pan in which the peppers were frying and fry the chicken pieces until golden brown.

Once the chicken is cooked, place it in the dish with the peppers and mushrooms.

Combine the cold water, cornflour and non-dairy creamer, and mix well. Pour into a large saucepan and bring to the boil, stirring with a whisk as you do so. As it starts to thicken, reduce the heat and add the peppers, mushrooms and chicken, stirring gently.

Add salt and pepper to taste.

At this point I like to place the mixture into the fridge so that it can absorb all the flavours. Ten minutes before you're ready to eat, cook the pasta according to the instructions on the packet and warm up the sauce. If you feel the sauce is a little too thick, add a little boiled pasta water to thin it down a bit.

Serve the pasta and sauce separately as some people like more sauce than pasta and vice versa! Grind black pepper on top and garnish with flat-leaf parsley.

SERVES 4

smoked CHICKEN, MUSHROOM AND LEEK PIE

NOT KNOWING WHAT LIES BENEATH THAT LID OF GOLDEN PUFF PASTRY ALLOWS PIES TO BE WRAPPED UP IN THEIR OWN MYSTERIOUS DELIGHT. AND THIS PIE IS NO DIFFERENT IN THAT IT IS NOT A BORING OLD CHICKEN AND MUSHROOM PIE, BUT A TASTE SENSATION ALL OF ITS OWN.

1 smoked chicken or leftover smoked turkey
3 leeks, chopped
1 onion, chopped
2 Tbsp finely chopped fresh parsley
2 cloves garlic, crushed
little oil for frying
1 Tbsp cornflour dissolved in ½ cup cold water
250 g fresh mushrooms, sliced
2 cups chicken stock or 2 chicken stock cubes dissolved in 2 cups boiling water
½ cup non-dairy creamer or Orley Whip™
1 x 400 g roll puff pastry
1 egg yolk and 1 Tbsp water, lightly beaten with a fork

Preheat the oven to 200 °C. Debone the chicken and cut into bite-size pieces.

Fry the leeks, onion, parsley and garlic in a little oil.

While the vegetables are frying, dissolve the cornflour in the ½ cup cold water.

When the vegetables are soft, add the mushrooms and fry until most of the moisture evaporates.

Add the stock, dissolved cornflour and non-dairy creamer and leave to simmer until it thickens.

Add the diced chicken and leave to heat through.

Divide the pastry in half and roll it out, thin enough to line a pie dish with the one piece, and cover the pie when filled with the other. (If preferred, make small, individual pies.)

Fill the lining with the chicken filling and cover with pastry. Trim off the edges and paint the pastry lid with egg wash. If you want to freeze this pie and use it another day, place it in the freezer at this point. When ready to use, defrost and bake.

Bake at 180 °C for 30–45 minutes or until golden brown.

Serve with mashed potato and peas.

Note: Remember, the meat and vegetables are already cooked; all you're doing is heating it through and baking the pastry.

SERVES 6

CHICKEN PASTA
laced with garlic and basil pesto

THIS DISH IS NOT A PASTA DISH SOAKED IN SAUCE, BUT RATHER A DELICATELY LACED PASTA DISH WITH A WONDERFUL ITALIAN FLAVOUR!

1 x 35 g packet fresh basil leaves
1 x 35 g packet fresh flat-leaf parsley
6 cloves garlic, crushed
2 fresh red chillies (optional)
½ cup olive oil
½ cup pine nuts
1 kg chicken stir-fry
salt and pepper
little olive oil for frying
250 g ribbon noodles
1 Tbsp non-dairy margarine

Roughly chop the basil and parsley before putting them in the food processor, otherwise the long stalks can get caught up in the blade. Place the garlic, chillies, basil, parsley and olive oil in the food processor. Pulse it a couple of times so that all the ingredients are well combined.

Add the pine nuts and pulse it a few more times. Place the pesto into a bowl and set aside.

Season the chicken with salt and pepper to taste. Fry small batches of chicken at a time until golden brown.

As you start frying the last batch of chicken, cook the pasta according to the instructions on the box.

When the pasta is ready, drain off the water and place the pasta back into the pot. Add the margarine and allow it to melt into the hot pasta. Add the chicken and pesto and put it back onto the stove on low heat. Cover and leave it to heat through for a few minutes.

Make sure it doesn't burn on the bottom – either shake the pot or gently lift the pasta with two forks to aerate it.

Season with salt and ground black pepper and serve immediately.

SERVES 4–6

'And the rabbi said ...'

DELI
delights

THE DON'TS OF HOT DOG EATING!

- Don't ever think that there's a wrong time to eat a hot dog!
- Don't boil Viennas, as the sausages are already cooked – once the water starts boiling, place the sausages into the water and switch off the heat allowing them to heat through.
- Don't turn over or lift a Vienna out of a pot with a fork as this pricks the skin and all the flavour runs out. Use tongs only.
- Don't put tomato sauce on the roll, put it on the sausage!
- Don't eat hot dogs with a knife and fork – only with your hands!
- Don't take more than five bites to finish a hot dog!
- Don't use a serviette – lick the tomato sauce and mustard off your fingers!
- Don't think you can't serve a hot dog to everyone, you can! American presidents have served kings hot dogs at the White House!
- Don't call a hot dog by its original name. I believe the 't' is now silent and they are now referred to as 'hoddogs'.

Ian's 'fantasy' HOT DOGS

EVERYBODY HAS THEIR OWN WAY OF PREPARING A HOT DOG. SOME LIKE THE SAUSAGE BOILED, OTHERS GRILLED; SOME LIKE THE ROLLS SOFT, OTHERS CRISPY. BUT QUITE 'FRANKLY', THIS IS MY HUSBAND IAN'S VERSION. NO PLATES, NO KNIVES, NO FORKS, JUST A PAIR OF TONGS AND GREASEPROOF PAPER PACKETS! IF HE HAD TO START LOOKING FOR CUTLERY AND CROCKERY, WE WOULDN'T EVER GET TO ENJOY HIS HOT DOGS!

sufficient frankfurters or Viennas to go around
sufficient pre-cut rolls for your frankfurters/Viennas
mayonnaise (squeeze bottle)
pickled cucumbers, thinly sliced
tomato sauce (squeeze bottle)
mustard sauce (squeeze bottle)

Place the sausages into a pot of boiling water and switch off the heat. The secret is not to boil the sausages, as they may burst and their wonderful flavour will escape into the water.

Squeeze mayonnaise onto both sides of a pre-cut hot dog roll (any design you like!). Place a few cucumber slices on top of the mayonnaise on the base of the hot dog roll.

Place a sausage on top of the cucumbers, squeeze tomato sauce and mustard over the top and place into a greaseproof paper packet. Bite into the hot dog and imagine that you're at Anfield watching Liverpool thrashing Manchester United. Nothing could be better for Ian, both the taste and the image!

153 | DELI DELIGHTS

BUBBLE AND SQUEAK LATKES
with crispy macon

BUBBLE AND SQUEAK IS SOMETHING QUITE UNIQUE. IT COMBINES POTATO AND CABBAGE LIKE A TRAVELLER AND HIS BAGGAGE! YOU JUST CAN'T TELL BECAUSE IT BLENDS SO WELL!

6 large potatoes
½ head large cabbage, thickly shredded
3 large onions, chopped
2 x 250 g packets beef macon, diced into small pieces
1 tsp chicken stock powder
2 eggs, well beaten
½ cup flour
salt and pepper
2 cups fine breadcrumbs or crushed cornflakes
oil for frying

Peel and quarter the potatoes and boil in salted water until soft.

Boil the cabbage for ±10 minutes in 1 cup water, covered, until soft but not mushy.

While the potatoes are boiling, fry the onions and diced macon together until crispy (don't trim off the fat). Remove from the heat and set aside.

Drain all the water off the potatoes and mash well (they shouldn't be velvety smooth).

Drain the cabbage well through a strainer. Add the cabbage to the mashed potatoes. Mix thoroughly, then add the onions and macon.

Add the stock powder to the beaten eggs and pour into the potato mixture. Mix thoroughly and add the flour, and salt and pepper to taste.

Roll the mixture into balls (slightly bigger than golf balls), roll them in the breadcrumbs, then press them slightly flatter to resemble burger patties. Fry in shallow oil until golden brown and drain on brown paper.

Note: These can be reheated in the oven, uncovered, for about 10–15 minutes at 180 °C.

MAKES 15–20

rare roast
BRUSCHETTAS

WE WENT TO VISIT MY SON WHO WAS STUDYING AT A YESHIVA IN NEW YORK. WE DECIDED THAT WE WERE GOING TO EXPERIENCE THE NEW YORK NIGHTLIFE WITH 'GUSTO', OR SO WE THOUGHT! AS IT TURNED OUT, WE WENT TO BED EARLY, EXHAUSTED FROM EATING, LIKE BLOATED 'GUTSOS'! WHY? BECAUSE WE HAD TO EXPERIENCE EVERY KOSHER RESTAURANT, DELI AND TAKE-AWAY WE WALKED PAST! HOW COULD A BUTCHER WALK PAST A DELI AND NOT TRY THEIR MEAT? IF THERE WAS ONE MEAL I WAS DETERMINED TO RECREATE, IT WAS THIS ONE. I PICKED AT THE WAITRESS'S BRAIN UNTIL I MANAGED TO GET WHAT I NEEDED OUT OF HER!

2 large tomatoes, finely chopped
1 large onion, finely chopped
1 x 35 g packet fresh basil leaves, chopped
salt and pepper
8–10 thin slices of baguette, cut diagonally
½ cup oil infused with 1 tsp crushed garlic and pinch salt
1 avocado (when in season)
250 g sliced rare roast beef, cut into thin strips or bite-size pieces

Preheat the oven to 180 °C. Combine the tomatoes, onion, basil, and salt and pepper to taste. This can be made a few hours in advance and refrigerated.

Place the sliced bread on a baking tray and paint each slice with the garlic oil. Bake in the oven on the middle rack until golden brown. You could also paint and brown them on a ridged skillet on top of the stove – they wouldn't be as crunchy and dry, but some people prefer them this way. When the bread is ready, remove it from the oven and leave to cool. It should be dry and crispy.

Just before assembling, pour off any excess juice that has accumulated in the tomato and onion mixture.

TO SERVE:
The New Yorkers serve their bruschettas with a layer of mashed avocado, followed by a layer of tomato and onion, topped with shredded rare roast. Shredding the meat makes it easier to eat as slices can be difficult to bite through.

Notes: I've also used turkey breast with a garlic aïoli sauce (see page 165) instead of rare roast successfully. In America they serve huge portions. They serve three on a plate (their bread is sliced thinly, but very long along the diagonal). It all depends on the size of your slices, and whether you're serving the bruschettas small as cocktails or large for a deli dinner.

SERVES 8–10

156   DELI DELIGHTS

CORN DOGS

ON MY FIRST-EVER VISIT TO AMERICA, I DISCOVERED CORN DOGS! OH DEAR, WHY DID I HAVE TO TRY THESE DEEP-FRIED, CORN-BATTERED SAUSAGES? I NOW MAKE SURE THAT I DROP A FEW KILOGRAMS BEFORE I GO TO VISIT THE FAMILY, ONLY SO THAT I CAN PUT THE WEIGHT BACK ON IN CORN DOGS!

2 egg yolks, lightly beaten
1¾ cups water
1 cup mealie meal
1 tsp bicarbonate of soda
1 cup self-raising flour
1½ tsp salt
4 cups oil
18–20 cocktail Viennas
18–20 wooden kebab sticks

Place the egg yolks and water into a food processor. Add the mealie meal, bicarbonate of soda, flour and salt, and beat or blend until smooth.

Place the batter into a round bowl, deep enough to dip an entire sausage into.

Preheat the oil in a deep pot or fryer. Rather use a smaller pot but one that is deep, as the entire batter-dipped sausage on a stick must be immersed into the oil. If the pot is too big, you'll need much more oil, as the entire length of the sausage needs to be immersed in the oil.

Pat the sausages dry with paper towel (they need to be dry so that the batter will stick to them).

Take a kebab stick and push it lengthwise into the cocktail sausage. Holding it upside down, cover the entire sausage in batter. Allow some of the batter to drip off the tip.

Still holding it by the end of the stick, gently immerse the sausage into the hot oil and fry until golden brown. The stick needs to be long to avoid getting yourself burnt by the bubbling oil.

Repeat with the remaining sausages. Fry one at a time as you need to keep turning them while they fry.

These are delicious plain or with mustard and tomato sauce.

MAKES 18–20

cowboy COUNTRY COOK-IN

THERE'S SOMETHING SPECIAL ABOUT A WINTER'S NIGHT ON A FARM – EVERYBODY WRAPPED IN BLANKETS, SITTING ON HAY BALES, HUDDLED AROUND A CRACKLING FIRE, EATING SAUSAGES AND BEANS AS THE SUN SETS ON AN UNINTERRUPTED VIEW OF THE LAND.

1 x 500 g packet Vienna sausages
1 x 500 g packet Russian sausages
2 onions, cut in half and sliced
into semi-circles
little oil for frying
½ cup water
2 cloves garlic, crushed
1 x 450 g tin baked beans in
tomato sauce
1 x 450 g tin beans in chilli sauce
1 Tbsp finely chopped
fresh flat-leaf parsley

Cut the Viennas and Russians into bite-size pieces and fry with the onions in a little oil until golden brown. Add the water and give it a good stir.

Add the garlic, both tins of beans and the parsley, and leave to simmer.

TO SERVE:
This can be served with mealie meal mixed with a tin of cream-style sweetcorn and a chunk of bread for dunking. For that real cowboy effect, serve on aluminium plates!

SERVES 8

GLAZED POLONY
in mini pita

THIS HAS BECOME A REGULAR FRIDAY NIGHT FEATURE IN OUR HOME. THE CHILDREN LOVE IT (AND MOST OF THE ADULTS TOO). IT'S ALMOST AS IF IT HAS TO BE SERVED STANDARD WITH ANY ROAST!

1 kg garlic polony
¾ cup tomato sauce
1 cup mild chutney
½ cup sweet chilli sauce
1 Tbsp mild peri-peri sauce
1 roll aluminium foil
3 packets mini pitas

Preheat the oven to 190 °C. Remove the covering and slice the polony into 0.5 cm slices – not all the way through, but just as you would slice garlic bread, three-quarters of the way down.

Mix the tomato sauce, chutney, sweet chilli and peri-peri sauces, and place a teaspoonful between each slice of polony. Wrap the polony up in foil, place on a baking tray and bake for 1 hour. When baked, open up the foil and baste the polony with the sauce that has leaked around the sides. Return it to the oven with the foil unwrapped until the polony crisps a little around the edges, but is still moist.

Cut each pita about three-quarters of the way through so that it is still sealed on one side.

Remove the polony from the oven and cut each slice through. Place one slice of polony into each mini pita or, alternatively, put the whole polony on a platter with a knife and arrange the pita bread around it.

SERVES 10

PITA PATTA
pass-arounds

THIS IS SOMETHING 'YOU CAN NEVER MAKE ENOUGH OF'! PASS THEM AROUND WITH CHOPPED LIVER, AVOCADO, BRINJAL, OR ANY OTHER KIND OF DIP. I ALSO CRUSH THEM OVER SALADS AS AN ALTERNATIVE TO CROUTONS!

6 cloves garlic, crushed
½ cup oil
6 pitas
garlic salt

Preheat the oven to 200 °C. Combine the crushed garlic and oil in a glass bowl. Cut a pita in half so that you have two full circles. Cut each circle into quarters (8 triangles). Do the same with all the pitas.

Place the pita triangles onto a well-greased baking tray. Paint each one with the garlic oil and sprinkle lightly with garlic salt. Bake for 8–15 minutes until golden brown. Store in an airtight container.

MAKES 48

DELI DELIGHTS

RARE ROAST BAGUETTES
with red onion marmalade

I ALWAYS HAVE A COUPLE OF BAGS OF RARE ROAST IN GRAVY IN MY FREEZER, JUST IN CASE! WHETHER YOU SERVE IT FORMALLY WITH VEGETABLES OR INFORMALLY IN A BAGUETTE, IT'S GOT TO HAVE THE ONION MARMALADE. IT TAKES THE MEAT AND TURNS IT INTO A MAGICAL MOMENT! WHAT'S EVEN MORE DELICIOUS IS WHEN THE GRAVY 'SQUOOSHES' OUT THE SIDES OF THE BAGUETTE.

±20 slices rare roast beef in gravy (4 slices per person)
1 large baguette (maybe 2, depending on the number of people)

FOR THE RED ONION MARMALADE
5 red onions, sliced
¾ cup soft brown treacle sugar
little oil for frying
¼ cup balsamic vinegar
1 tsp peri-peri sauce (medium or hot) (optional)
salt and pepper

BUILDING THE BAGUETTE:
Heat the rare roast in gravy, either in the microwave or simply drop the vacuum bag into boiling water to heat through.

Slice the baguette in half lengthwise. Make up the whole baguette, then slice into smaller pieces or cut the baguette up and make individual ones.

Place the sliced beef onto the bread, spread onion marmalade over the top and spoon some gravy from the roast over the meat.

RED ONION MARMALADE:
Fry the onions and sugar in a large frying pan with a little oil until limp. Keep stirring until they start to brown.

Reduce the heat, then add the vinegar, peri-peri sauce, salt and pepper to taste, and leave to simmer for 10–15 minutes or until a thick glaze coats the onions.

Switch off the heat, cover and leave it to stew in its own juice!

The onion marmalade can be made in advance and reheated. It should keep in the fridge for at least a week before using.

MAKES 4 OR 5

Hymie's HOME-MADE SAUSAGE ROLLS

THERE'S A BUZZ AT THE DOOR AND, AS YOU ANSWER IT, SOMEBODY BELLOWS DOWN THE MOUTHPIECE, 'IS THAT THE BEST SAUSAGE ROLL MAKER IN TOWN?' AND YOU KNOW YOU'VE GOT YOUR WORK CUT OUT FOR THE AFTERNOON, 'CAUSE UNCLE HYMIE AIN'T GOING HOME UNTIL HE'S HAD HIS SAUSAGE ROLLS!

1 x 500 g packet breakfast sausages
1 tsp dried sage (this is the secret!)
½ cup breadcrumbs
½ cup cold water
1 x 400 g packet puff pastry

Preheat the oven to 190 °C. Peel off the sausage skins or squeeze the sausage meat out of its casing. Place into a bowl, add the sage, breadcrumbs and water, and mix well.

Roll out the pastry into a rectangular shape about 2 mm thick on a lightly floured, flat surface.

Place a row of sausage meat lengthwise along the edge of the pastry and roll the pastry over it once like a Swiss roll, ensuring that the meat is completely covered with pastry. Roll it gently with both hands, cut into bite-size pieces or a little bigger, if you prefer, and place the sausage rolls 'seam' side down on a baking tray. Repeat until you've used up all the meat.

Paint with egg wash (1 egg lightly beaten with ¼ cup water), cut a slit in the top of the pastry and bake in the oven until golden brown.

MAKES ±12–15 (COCKTAIL SIZE)

RYE TURKEY TOWER
with aïoli and horseradish sauce

TURKEY BREAST JUST HAPPENS TO BE MY FAVOURITE COLD MEAT AND FOR ME THERE'S NOTHING NICER THAN TOWERING SLICED TURKEY ON SOFT, FRESH RYE BREAD WITH LASHINGS OF AÏOLI SAUCE. IT'S A 'SARMIE' FOR ALL SEASONS, SUMMER OR WINTER – IN WINTER I WARM UP THE AÏOLI SAUCE AND IN SUMMER I LEAVE IT COOL!

1 loaf rye bread, pre-sliced
schmaltz and/or mustard sauce
500 g white turkey pastrami
2 tomatoes, thinly sliced
1 large onion, thinly sliced
pickled cucumbers

**FOR THE AÏOLI AND
HORSERADISH SAUCE**
2 egg yolks
1 Tbsp prepared mustard or
1 tsp mustard powder
1 cup olive oil
1 Tbsp white vinegar
1 tsp freshly grated white
horseradish
5 cloves garlic, crushed
½ tsp salt and ¼ tsp pepper

Take two slices of rye bread and spread with schmaltz or a thin layer of mustard sauce (or both!). On one slice, build up a delicious tower with turkey, sliced tomatoes, onions, cucumbers and the aïoli sauce. Place the other slice on top and have fun! Serve extra aïoli sauce on the side.

AÏOLI AND HORSERADISH SAUCE:
Place the egg yolks and mustard into a food processor and blend well. (If you don't have a food processor, whisk it by hand.)

While blending, add the oil drop by drop and, as it starts to thicken, start trickling it in, in a thin stream.

When you have added all the oil, add the vinegar, horseradish, garlic, salt and pepper, give it a minute longer to combine, then store in the fridge.

The aïoli sauce can be warmed up either in the microwave or on top of the stove.

SERVES 4

breakfast muffin
MACON POTS

MY CHILDREN CREATED THIS FOR US ON ONE OF OUR ANNIVERSARIES. HOWEVER, THE STORY IS AS DELICIOUS AS THE BREAKFAST! ONE CHILD SUGGESTED TOMATO AND ONION OMELETTES, THE OTHER MACON AND EGGS, AND THE OTHER MUFFINS. NATURALLY AN ARGUMENT ENSUED UNTIL MY DAUGHTER SUGGESTED THEY COMBINE ALL THREE IDEAS AND THIS IS WHAT THEY CREATED.

1 large onion, chopped
2 medium tomatoes, chopped
12–14 slices macon
6 eggs
salt and pepper

Preheat the oven to 240 °C (very high heat). Fry the onion until soft, then add the tomatoes and simmer for about 5 minutes. Keep stirring to prevent sticking.

Grease a muffin tray (six-cup, deep muffin tray) and line each muffin cup with two slices of macon, one running one way and the other across.

Make sure the meat is pressed firmly against the sides of the cup and drapes over the top.

Place a spoonful of the tomato and onion mixture on top of the meat in each cup. Crack an egg into a small glass bowl, then gently pour it over the top of the tomato and onion mixture.

Bake on the middle shelf of the oven until the egg whites are firm and the macon becomes crisp. Reduce the heat if you think the meat is burning, but remember that the eggs take a little longer to cook through – they probably need about 15 minutes, depending, of course, on your oven.

Gently remove each muffin from the muffin tin and serve immediately with toasted health bread and a glass of fresh orange juice.

MAKES 6

'Is it too late to tell them that I don't eat meat?'

ON THE SIDE *a little*

As insects are not kosher, fruit and vegetables need to be checked thoroughly. Due to the strict rules of washing and checking fruit and vegetables, a worm gazing up at you from a lettuce leaf asking for directions, is definitely a no-no in a kosher home!

The Principal Rabbinical Supervisor of the Kashrut Department of the Johannesburg Beth Din, Rabbi Yossi Baumgarten, has produced a comprehensive guide to cleaning and checking fruit and vegetables. I would suggest you download it from the Internet on www.uos.co.za, laminate it and keep it in an easily accessible spot in your kitchen.

FARM FRESH GREEN BEANS
with macon and crispy onions

OH BOY, DID WE GET A CROP OF GREEN BEANS ONE YEAR ON MY PARENTS' FARM! SO IT WAS GREEN BEANS AT EVERY MEAL. TO THIS DAY MY BROTHER WON'T EAT ANY GREEN VEGETABLES, NEVER MIND BEANS!

250 g packet macon
little oil for frying
500 g fresh green beans, topped
and tailed, then cut in half
pinch salt
1 x 40 g packet crispy
onion pieces (Osem™ are kosher)

Slice the macon into thin strips across the grain of the meat. Fry in a little oil (just enough to cover the bottom of the frying pan) until the fat on the meat turns glossy. Remove from the heat.

To the same pan (do not add any more oil) add the beans and a pinch of salt, and fry for about 5 minutes, tossing continuously. Place the meat back into the pan, switch off the heat, cover and leave for a while (the beans must not be fried until soft).

When ready to serve, heat through for a minute or two, place into a serving dish and sprinkle with the crispy onions.

SERVES 8–10

crispy BUTTERNUT BLINTZES

EVER WONDERED WHO BUYS THOSE HUGE BAGS OF BUTTERNUT, EVEN WHEN THEY'RE NOT ON SPECIAL? WELL, TRY THIS RECIPE AND YOU'LL NEVER WALK PAST THOSE BAGS AGAIN.

3 kg butternut
1 x 200 ml packet curry sauce
(Ina Paarman's™ is kosher)
salt and pepper
1 x 500 g box phyllo pastry

Peel and cut the butternut into small pieces and boil in 1 cup water. Butternut creates its own liquid while cooking, but it does evaporate quickly, so keep an eye on it.

When all the water has evaporated, mash the butternut and leave it to cool. It should not be watery, as it will ooze from the pastry when you bake it.

Add the curry sauce and blend either with a hand blender or mash until smooth. Add salt and pepper to taste.

Preheat the oven to 180 °C. Unroll the phyllo pastry and work with one sheet at a time, keeping the remaining sheets covered with the plastic foil in which they come wrapped.

Place the pastry on a flat surface, cut each piece in half and place a spoonful of butternut one-third of the way down on each piece. Fold the sides in to meet in the middle and roll the pastry up like a Swiss roll.

Place on an oiled baking tray and spray each blintze with olive oil spray. Repeat until all the butternut or phyllo has been used up, whichever first!

At this point, the blintzes can be frozen before being baked. I normally bake as many as I need for the night and freeze the rest.

Bake for about 15 minutes until golden brown and serve immediately with your favourite ready-made tomato salsa.

Notes: If you are using ready-peeled and cut butternut, you will only need 2 kg.

I have successfully combined leftover mashed potato with butternut in this recipe and added a tin of creamed sweetcorn just for fun, and that was great too!

MAKES 25–28

A LITTLE ON THE SIDE

ASPARAGUS STICKS
and couscous crunch

THE COUSCOUS CRUNCH IS A WONDERFUL, CRUNCHY TOPPING FOR SO MANY DISHES. ITS NEUTRAL TASTE ALLOWS YOU TO DO SO MUCH WITH IT. I SPRINKLE IT ON LAMB, ASPARAGUS, GREEN BEANS, PUMPKIN AND WHATEVER I THINK NEEDS CRUNCHING UP.

2 trays fresh green asparagus

FOR THE COUSCOUS CRUNCH
1 cup couscous
garlic-flavoured olive oil spray

FOR THE GARLIC 'BUTTER'
1 tsp finely crushed garlic or
½ tsp garlic salt
2 Tbsp non-dairy margarine

Preheat the oven to 190 °C. Place the couscous onto a baking tray and spray liberally with olive oil. Bake for 10 minutes or until golden brown. Watch it, as it browns quickly.

Place a large pot on the stove and half fill with salted water. Bring to the boil and drop the asparagus into the boiling water.

Place the lid on the pot to cover the asparagus and boil for 8–10 minutes. Remove from the heat and drain off all the water.

To make the garlic 'butter', melt together the crushed garlic or garlic salt, and the margarine. Place the asparagus on a baking tray, drizzle with garlic 'butter' and bake in a preheated oven at 190 °C for 8–10 minutes.

Remove, sprinkle with couscous crunch and serve immediately. If you don't use all the couscous crunch, put whatever is left into an airtight bag and freeze.

Notes: If you're pressed for time, use tinned green asparagus. Drain off the liquid and skip the boiling process. Place them straight into the preheated oven, drizzle with garlic 'butter' and heat through for about 10 minutes.

Fresh asparagus need to be washed very well to get rid of any sandy bits.

SERVES 3–4 PER PERSON WHEN SERVED AS AN ACCOMPANIMENT TO A MEAT DISH, MORE IF SERVED AS A STARTER

string of PEARL ONIONS

SOME PEOPLE SAY PEARLS BRING TEARS. WELL, THE ONLY TEARS YOU'LL GET FROM THIS STRING IS WHEN YOU PEEL THEM! THEY'RE SO SIMPLE, SO DELICIOUS, AND JUST SO TASTY!

oil for frying
1 kg pearl onions, peeled
pinch salt
2 Tbsp soft brown treacle sugar
1 cup red wine

Heat a little oil in a large frying pan. Add the onions, sprinkle with a little salt and allow them to brown. Keep moving them around and turning them over to prevent them from burning in one spot.

Reduce the heat and add the sugar, stirring as you do. Make sure all the onions are coated with the dissolved sugar and continue to stir and move them about as they cook. Simmer for about 5 minutes, stirring continuously, as they burn quite quickly.

Increase the heat, add the red wine and bring it to the boil. Continue stirring the onions ensuring that they are well coated. Reduce the heat and simmer for a few more minutes.

Switch off the heat, cover the frying pan with a lid and leave the onions to relax and absorb the flavours. Reheat when ready to serve.

SERVES 8–10

A FEW POTATO IDEAS

MY CHILDREN ARE MEAT AND POTATO ADDICTS, AND BELIEVE THAT THE TWO GO TOGETHER LIKE A HORSE AND CARRIAGE! SO, TO KEEP THINGS RUNNING SMOOTHLY, 'POTATO ANXIETY PREVENTION' IS NECESSARY. I AM THEREFORE ALWAYS ON THE LOOKOUT FOR NEW POTATO IDEAS. HERE ARE A FEW THAT KEEP THEM SATISFIED!

mashed ONION POTATOES

I USE THESE MASHED ONION POTATOES AS A BASE FOR QUITE A FEW POTATO DISHES.

6 large potatoes, peeled and cubed
2 Tbsp onion soup powder
1 Tbsp non-dairy margarine
salt and pepper

Boil the potatoes in a pot with just enough water to cover. When the potatoes are soft and most of the water has evaporated, leaving the potatoes looking moist, add the onion soup mix, stir and leave the potatoes to continue boiling for a further 5 minutes. (If you add the onion soup before the potatoes have had a chance to soften, it will take longer for them to soften.)

Once most of the liquid has evaporated, mash the potatoes, switch off the heat, add the non-dairy margarine, salt and pepper, and leave the potatoes to stand, covered, for about 10 minutes.

Reheat on top of the stove or in the microwave.

SERVES 6

potato CRACKERS

If you want to make mash a little more elegant, take a sheet of phyllo pastry and cut it in half lengthwise. Preheat the oven to 180 °C. Place 2 tablespoons of Mashed Onion Potatoes on the top third of the pastry. Spread it out a little, but ensure that you leave a 3–4 cm margin along both sides of the pastry. Don't fold in the sides, just roll them up and twist each end to produce a cracker effect. Spray with olive oil spray and place each cracker onto a pre-oiled baking tray. Bake until golden brown. These cannot be warmed up in the microwave, so bake just before serving.

MAKES 6–8

savoury POTATO MUFFINS

½ cup boiling water

2 cups Mashed Onion Potatoes (page 175)

2 eggs, lightly beaten

¾ cup flour, sifted

1 heaped tsp baking powder

salt and pepper

Preheat the oven to 180 °C. Add the boiling water to the Mashed Onion Potatoes to help soften the mixture, then add the beaten eggs and mix well. Add the sifted flour, baking powder, and salt and pepper to taste, and mix well. Spoon the mixture into a well-greased muffin tray. Bake for 30 minutes or until golden brown.

You could also fry spoonfuls in a lightly oiled frying pan. Take a heaped tablespoon of the mixture, place it in the pan and flatten slightly with a spatula so that the mounds are about 2 cm thick. They don't have to be perfectly round, smooth or the same size. Cook until brown on the bottom, turn over and fry the other side.

SERVES 6–8

Russian HASH BROWNS

6 large potatoes

2 large onions, chopped

little oil for frying

7–8 Russian sausages

salt and pepper

Preheat the oven to 170 °C. Boil the potatoes, with the skin on, until just soft (not falling apart) or bake in the microwave until soft. Remove from the pot and leave to cool. Meanwhile, fry the onions until soft and glassy.

Slice the sausages in half and roughly dice them up. Skin the potatoes and cut into small cubes. Add the onions and diced sausage, and fold together gently. Add salt and pepper to taste.

Heat a lightly oiled frying pan and fry about 1 cup of the mixture at a time. Allow it to go dark and golden brown in colour, then place in the oven until the rest have been fried.

Notes: Instead of frying it in batches, you could also place the mixture onto an oiled baking tray and bake for 45–60 minutes at 180 °C until golden brown. Cut it into slices or squares when ready.

SERVES 6–8

POTATO AND ONION
sticks

THESE ARE REALLY TASTY, AND JUST SEEM TO GO HAND IN HAND WITH LAMB. HOWEVER, I SOMETIMES PAINT THEM WITH EGGPLANT DIP (CAN BE PURCHASED READY MADE AT MOST SUPERMARKETS) WHEN I MAKE THE MEDITERRANEAN-STYLE VEAL.

1 kg baby potatoes, unpeeled
1 kg baby onions
1 packet kebab sticks

FOR THE BASTING SAUCE
½ cup olive oil
¼ cup soy sauce
1 tsp paprika
1 tsp crushed garlic
1 tsp salt
2 tsp grainy prepared mustard
1 tsp dried rosemary
1 Tbsp onion soup powder
1 x 250 g tub eggplant dip
(optional)

Thread a potato followed by an onion onto a kebab stick and repeat this all the way down the stick until you have about 4 cm free at the bottom (to hold the stick). There should be three of each vegetable, but it also depends on their size. You can also cut the vegetables in half if you prefer. Place the kebabs side by side (not on top of one another) into a large roasting pan.

BASTING SAUCE:
Preheat the oven to 180 °C. Make up the basting sauce by combining all the ingredients, except the eggplant dip. Paint each kebab well, ensuring that all the basting sauce is used.

Roast in the oven for about 45 minutes until brown and crispy (depending on their size). Turn them over and roast for a further 30 minutes. At this point paint the kebabs with eggplant dip, if using.

If you feel they are browning too quickly, turn the heat down a little. I have also placed them, quite successfully, in the microwave to soften them, then basted them and left them to marinate for a while, then browned them on the braai/barbecue.

MAKE 1 PER PERSON

Aunt Freida's Original Salad Dr

'Bobba's secret salad dressing ...'

LEAF
me alone

standby ANTIPASTO PLATTER

EVER HAD THOSE AFTERNOONS WHEN YOU'RE HAVING SO MUCH FUN WITH YOUR FRIENDS THAT YOU DON'T WANT THE DAY TO END? WELL, IT DOESN'T HAVE TO, JUST BRING OUT THE ANTIPASTO PLATTER. IT TAKES JUST A FEW MINUTES TO PREPARE, AS MOST OF THE INGREDIENTS ARE EITHER TINNED OR IN THE FRIDGE! SO, HERE'S A LIST OF STANDBY INGREDIENTS TO PREVENT IT FROM BECOMING AN ANTISOCIAL PLATTER!

1 head butter lettuce
2 x 250 g packets continental salami
2 x 450 g tins large asparagus
250 g ready-made brinjal salad
250 g ready-made techina
1 x 200 g packet button mushrooms, washed and marinated in Italian salad dressing
1 x 740 g bottle pickled cucumbers
1 x 250 g packet rosa tomatoes
10–15 black olives
10–15 green olives
1 x 450 g tin artichoke hearts, drained and marinated in a bottle of Italian salad dressing
1 x 420 g bottle pickled piquanté peppers
2 medium avocados
1 x 250 g packet carrots, julienne style
1 x 200 g tray fresh baby corn
1 x 200 g packet sugar snap peas
toasted bagel chips
ciabatta bread
… and anything else you may want to add!

Cover a platter with a layer of butter lettuce.

Wrap a slice of salami around an asparagus, using a toothpick to secure it.

Section off the platter into V's, so that the point of the V is in the centre. Combine the brinjal and techina in a bowl, place in the centre of the platter and work outwards from that point.

Create a section for the mushrooms, another for the cucumbers, another for the tomatoes, a section for the asparagus and salami, another for the olives, etc.

If there is anything on the platter that looks as if it needs a little help with moisture, shake up a bit of salad dressing and spoon it onto that section, e.g. the snap peas, baby tomatoes and baby corn may need help.

Serve with ciabatta bread, Pita Patta Pass-arounds (page 162) or bagel chips.

Note: Once a week, normally on Thursdays, I marinate a packet of mushrooms in Italian salad dressing, just to have around. Even if you don't serve an antipasto salad, serve them on their own or in another salad.

SERVES WHOEVER HASN'T GONE HOME!

5TH *avenue* DELI PICKLES

WHAT'S A DELI SANDWICH WITHOUT THE DELI PICKLES? IN NEW YORK, THE PICKLES ARRIVE BEFORE THE SANDWICH AND BY THE TIME THE SANDWICH ARRIVES, THEY KNOW TO BRING ANOTHER BOWL OF PICKLES! THERE WERE A COUPLE OF VEGETABLES IN SOME OF THOSE BOWLS OF PICKLES I WOULDN'T HAVE IMAGINED PUTTING TOGETHER, HOWEVER, THEY WORKED AND VERY WELL TOO!

FOR THE PICKLING VEGETABLES
1 small head cabbage
2 fresh English cucumbers
5 sticks celery
3 onions
1 x 250 g packet julienne-style carrots

FOR THE PICKLING JUICE
4 cups vinegar (1 litre)
12 cups water (3 litres)
¾ cup sugar
3 Tbsp salt
1 Tbsp whole peppercorns
8–10 cloves garlic, crushed (the finer you cut the garlic, the stronger the garlic flavour)
8 fresh or dried bay leaves

PICKLING VEGETABLES:

Wash and shred the cabbage (not too finely). Slice the cucumbers in half lengthwise, scoop out the pips with a teaspoon and cut on the diagonal into 5 mm slices. Wash and slice the celery on the diagonal into 5 mm slices. Cut the onions in half and slice into rings.

Place all the vegetables in a large bowl and mix together.

Fill the pickling jars seven-eighths full with vegetables. Cover completely with pickling juice and seal with a good sealing lid.

Place in the fridge and leave to pickle for a few days.

PICKLING JUICE:

Heat all the ingredients in a saucepan and bring to the boil. Once the sugar has dissolved, remove from the heat and set aside to cool.

Note: If you enjoy spicy food, add 2 hot chillies (the tiny red ones) to the pickling juice as well. Slice them in half lengthwise, seed them and add to the liquid before bringing it to the boil.

SERVES 10–12

TURKEY AND BERRY SALAD
with Bobba's ex-secret salad dressing

OK, SO NOW THE SECRET'S OUT! THE BEST THING ABOUT THIS SALAD IS DEFINITELY BOBBA'S DRESSING. HER RECIPE GOES BACK AT LEAST 25 YEARS. SHE MAKES IT BY THE GALLON AND THE FAMILY RECEIVES A FRESH BOTTLE EVERY FRIDAY – BELIEVE ME, IT DOESN'T LAST THE WEEK! NO MATTER HOW MANY SALAD DRESSINGS YOU PUT OUT, THERE'S ALWAYS SOMEONE AT THE TABLE WHO ASKS, 'GOT ANY OF BOBBA'S SALAD DRESSING?'.

**leftover smoked turkey or
1 smoked chicken
1 head butter lettuce
1 x 200 g packet sugar snap
peas, sliced in half horizontally
500 g berries (strawberries,
raspberries, blueberries,
cranberries, gooseberries –
whatever you can get, as long as
it ends in 'berries!)
handful craisons or sweetened,
dried cranberries
200 g caramelised nuts, crushed**

**FOR BOBBA'S SECRET DRESSING
1½ cups oil
1 cup white vinegar
1 cup brown sugar
½ tsp salt
½ cup mayonnaise
little ground pepper
2 tsp mustard powder
8 cloves garlic**

Cut the turkey into bite-size pieces. If using chicken, debone it and cut into pieces.

Arrange the butter lettuce on a platter, followed by the peas, berries and turkey or chicken.

Just before serving, cover in salad dressing, then sprinkle with crushed nuts.

BOBBA'S SECRET DRESSING:
Place all the ingredients in a liquidiser or food processor, or use a hand blender. Blend very well for a few minutes until well combined. Store in a glass bottle.

Note: The salad looks very effective with an assortment of berries. However, if you only have strawberries and tinned gooseberries, that's fine too!

SERVES 6

DRY WORS
salad

WE OFTEN MAKE SALADS THINKING, 'MMM … I WONDER HOW THIS WILL GO DOWN?' I THINK THE REASON THIS SALAD IS SUCH A SUCCESS IS THAT IT HAS SO MANY DIFFERENT TEXTURES AND TASTES, WHICH ALL COMBINE SO WELL. IT'S A SMOOTH, CRUNCHY, SPICY, SWEETISH, MILD, SOOTHING, AFRICAN KIND OF SALAD!

±10 baby potatoes
±10 baby onions
little peri-peri or olive oil for roasting
coarse salt
250 g baby tomatoes
little brown sugar for sprinkling
1 head butter lettuce or 1 x 500 g packet baby spinach
2 avocados
1 English cucumber, finely chopped
4 sticks dry wors (ask your butcher to shred the sticks) plus 2–4 whole dry wors sticks
1 x 410 g tin whole-kernel corn, drained
1 cup roasted corn (available at most health shops or supermarkets)

FOR THE SALAD DRESSING
½ cup brown vinegar
½ cup brown sugar
¼ cup oil
1 tsp prepared mustard
½ cup low-fat mayonnaise
salt and pepper

Steps one and two can be done in advance and set aside at room temperature for a few hours. Step three can only be done when you're ready to eat. However, it can be sliced and waiting!

STEP ONE:
Preheat the oven to 200 °C. Wash the baby potatoes well and slice in half (skin on). Peel the baby onions and cut them in half. Place the potatoes and onions in a roasting pan with a little oil and sprinkle with coarse salt. Roast in the oven for 30–40 minutes until golden brown.

STEP TWO:
Cut the baby tomatoes in half, sprinkle with a little brown sugar and place directly under the grill (as close as possible) on the highest shelf for 3–5 minutes, so that the sugar melts and they go a little black. Watch them constantly, as you don't want them to go mushy.

STEP THREE:
Arrange the butter lettuce or baby spinach on a platter, followed by the potatoes, onions, tomatoes, sliced avocado and chopped cucumber. Just before serving, pour the salad dressing over the salad and sprinkle with the dry wors, tinned corn and roasted corn.

SALAD DRESSING:
Blend the ingredients and pour over the salad when ready to serve.

Note: Here's something a little different: place two dry wors sticks on either side of the salad. When ready to toss the salad, use the sticks.

SERVES 6–8

LEAF ME ALONE

ITALIAN SALAD
and bolognaise twisters

MAKE THIS AND YOU'LL MAKE A STATEMENT!

FOR THE TWISTERS
200 g minced meat
little olive oil for frying
½ tsp crushed garlic
½ tsp dried Italian herbs
1 Tbsp tomato paste
salt and pepper
200 g (½ roll) puff pastry

FOR THE SALAD
1 x 30 g packet of rocket
1 head butter lettuce
6 jam or plain tomatoes,
roughly chopped
2 avocados
16 olives
2 red onions, cut in half and
sliced into rings
1 x 30 g packet basil leaves,
roughly chopped
1 x 250 ml bottle ready-made
Italian salad dressing
of your choice
½ cup toasted pine nuts

TWISTERS:

Preheat the oven to 180 °C. Fry the minced meat in a little oil, then add the garlic, Italian herbs and tomato paste, stirring continuously so that the mince doesn't go lumpy. Add salt and pepper to taste, and set aside to cool. (If you have any leftover Italian Beef Sauce, (page 103) use that instead of the minced meat.)

Roll the pastry out onto a lightly floured board. Spoon a thin layer of the mince evenly over the pastry. Gently roll the mince with a lightly oiled rolling pin into the pastry a few times in the same direction until you acquire a piece of pastry about 24 x 30 cm. The mince must be embedded in the pastry.

Cut the pastry into about six long strips and twist to spiral them. Bake, uncovered, on a baking tray for 15–20 minutes or until golden brown and crispy. Remove when baked and set aside.

Note: If you prefer not to use meat (why wouldn't you?), sprinkle dried garlic Italian herbs over the pastry and roll it into the pastry as you would the meat.

ASSEMBLING THE SALAD:

Place all the salad ingredients (except the dressing and pine nuts) in a large bowl and toss well. Just before serving, dress the salad with the dressing, toss it again and place onto a serving platter.

Arrange the twisters in a pile beside the salad or lattice them over the top of the salad. Sprinkle with the pine nuts and serve.

Notes: It's best to make the twisters about 30 minutes before serving so that they will still be crispy and have a chance to cool down a little. They can be made a few hours before and refrigerated, but will then have to be crisped up in the oven.

SERVES 8–10

crunchy Mexican
CARNE ENSALADA

AS ONE WHO ENJOYS DIFFERENT TEXTURES IN FOOD, THIS HAS IT ALL. IT CAN ALSO BE MADE WITH STRIPS OF CHICKEN, WHICH TASTES JUST AS GOOD.

1 large red onion, chopped
½ English cucumber, chopped
1 red pepper, chopped
2 medium tomatoes, chopped
2 sticks celery, roughly chopped
1 x 30 g packet fresh
coriander, chopped
2 tsp Mexican spice
½ tsp ground cumin
¾ cup plain flour
500 g beef strips (ask your
butcher to cut it shuwarma style)
oil for frying
1 lettuce, finely shredded
2 avocados, cubed
2 cups defrosted frozen corn or
1 x 410 g tin whole-kernel
corn, drained
1 x 150 g packet BBQ Fritos™ or
Big Corn Bites™ crisps

FOR THE SALAD DRESSING
½ cup oil
½ cup red wine vinegar
2 tsp mustard powder
4 cloves garlic
½ cup brown sugar
½ tsp paprika
½ cup ready-made salsa sauce
(available at most supermarkets)
salt and pepper

Place the chopped onion, cucumber, red pepper, tomatoes, celery and coriander into a bowl. Cover with half the salad dressing and allow to marinate for about an hour.

While this is marinating, combine the Mexican spice, cumin and flour. Sprinkle over the beef strips and mix so that they are well coated.

Fry small batches in a little oil until brown on both sides. Remove from the pan and set aside to cool.

When you're ready to serve the salad place the lettuce onto a platter, followed by the marinated salad ingredients, avocado, beef and corn.

Just before serving, pour the rest of the salad dressing over the salad and sprinkle with crushed corn crisps.

SALAD DRESSING:
Blend the ingredients with a hand blender or in a food processor.

Note: Something a little different. Place a layer of salad (with all the ingredients) on a tortilla (laffa), roll it up tightly and cut into 3 pieces. Secure with a toothpick and pass around as a cocktail.

SERVES 6

ROMAN-CE SALAD
with seeded crunchies

THIS WAS ONE OF THE SALADS WITH WHICH I USED TO TRY AND IMPRESS MY THEN BOYFRIEND (NOW HUSBAND). IT MUST HAVE IMPRESSED HIM MORE THAN I'D REALISED BECAUSE I DIDN'T KNOW THAT HE DIDN'T LIKE HARD-BOILED EGGS!

1 x 250 g packet smoked brisket or smoked steak
little oil for frying
3 hard-boiled eggs
1 health loaf (2 days old)
1 tsp dried Italian herbs
1 tsp garlic powder
oil for deep frying
1 tsp crushed garlic
1 x 500 g packet baby spinach

FOR THE SALAD DRESSING
½ cup sugar
½ cup oil
½ cup white vinegar
3 cloves garlic
1 cup mayonnaise
salt and pepper
1 tsp prepared grainy mustard

Chop the brisket into very small pieces, and fry in a little oil until crispy. Remove from the oil and drain on brown paper.

Shell the eggs and leave to cool, then coarsely grate into a bowl and set aside.

Cut off the first slice of the health loaf (crust) and, with your fingers, hollow out the inside of the loaf. Gently crumble the bread to form coarse bread crumbles. Sprinkle the herbs and garlic powder over the crumbles and mix well.

Heat the oil and garlic together, and add the crumbles in small batches. Watch carefully, as they brown quickly.

Remove with a slotted spoon and drain on brown paper. Repeat until all the crumbles have been fried. You need about 2 cups of fried crumbles. If you have any left over, place in an airtight container or plastic bag and freeze.

You can also bake the crumbles instead of frying them. Place them on a baking tray, sprinkle with garlic salt and Italian herbs, spray with olive oil spray and bake for 35–40 minutes at 150 °C until crispy.

Arrange the spinach on a salad platter followed by the grated eggs and fried brisket.

Just before serving, pour over the salad dressing. Finally, sprinkle with the bread crumbles.

SALAD DRESSING:
Combine all the ingredients with a hand blender or in a food processor, and blend until smooth.

SERVES 8

SANTORINI SALAD

MY FRIEND PAM WENT TO GREECE WITH THREE OF HER CHILDHOOD FRIENDS. THEY HAD MADE A PACT THAT NO MATTER WHERE THEY WERE LIVING, THE YEAR THAT THEY ALL TURNED 40, THEY WOULD MEET IN GREECE. SO IT WAS IN SANTORINI THAT THEY SWAM IN THE SEA, DRANK IN THE JACUZZI™ AND ATE SALAD FOR SUSTENANCE! IT WAS THE SALAD I WAS INTERESTED IN, SO WE GOT TO WORK, SUBSTITUTED HERE AND THERE, COULDN'T QUITE GET THE MOOD BACK FOR PAM, BUT WE FINALLY GOT THE TASTE!

2 fresh English cucumbers, chopped into bite-size pieces
350 g baby tomatoes
10 black olives
10 green olives
1 green pepper, roughly chopped
250 g smoked tofu, cubed into small pieces
1 white onion, cut in half and sliced into rings
1 red onion, cut in half and sliced into rings
1 cup couscous, baked in a hot oven at 200 °C until golden brown

FOR THE SALAD DRESSING
⅔ cup oil
¼ cup red wine vinegar
1 Tbsp sugar
½ tsp dried origanum
½ tsp ground black pepper
½ tsp salt
1 clove garlic, crushed

Place all the salad ingredients (except the couscous) into a bowl. Pour dressing over the salad and, just before serving, sprinkle with baked couscous.

SALAD DRESSING:
Place all the ingredients for the dressing in a small jar and shake well. Chill before serving.

ANOTHER SALAD DRESSING TO TRY:
½ cup mayonnaise
2 Tbsp hummus
½ cup water
¼ cup red wine vinegar
2 tsp sugar
½ tsp crushed garlic
pinch salt
twist or two ground black pepper

Place the ingredients in a small jar and shake well.

SERVES 8

African
SUNDOWNER SALAD

YOU DON'T NEED A WOODEN SUN DECK AND THE SUBTLE SOUND OF WATER RUNNING BENEATH YOU TO ENJOY THIS SALAD – BUT IT WOULD HELP! SO LET'S USE OUR WONDERFUL TRANSPORTATION SYSTEM CALLED THE IMAGINATION TO TAKE US THERE! HAVE FUN WITH THIS SALAD BY CREATING A LARGE, ROUND, VISUAL PLATTER OF AN AFRICAN SUNSET, USING ALL OUR MAGICAL-COLOURED FRUIT AND VEGETABLES.

1 head butter lettuce, roughly broken up into bite-size pieces
400 g smoked turkey breast (ask your butcher to cut it slightly thicker than cold meat)
1 large red onion, cut in half and finely sliced into rings
1 pineapple, peeled, cut in half and sliced into semicircular rings
2 oranges, peeled and segmented
2 red or pink grapefruit, peeled and segmented
1 large mango (or 1 x 450 g tin mango slices), peeled and thinly sliced lengthwise
1 small pawpaw, peeled, cut in half, seeds removed and sliced
1 small papino, cut the same way as the pawpaw
1 sweet red pepper, cut into fine strips lengthwise (to represent shimmering rays!)
pomegranate seeds (when in season) or granadilla pips

ASSEMBLING THE SALAD:

Arrange the butter lettuce on a platter. Slice the smoked turkey into thin strips and place on top of the lettuce, followed by the onion.

Now this is where the fun comes in because all the ingredients need to be placed in a circular fashion around the plate working from the middle outwards, trying to achieve a round, sunshine look!

Start with the pineapple as the inside circle, and gradually work your way outwards with the oranges, grapefruit, mango, pawpaw and papino (when in season, spanspek and watermelon can also be used).

Arrange the strips of red pepper from the centre outwards and finally add a few more turkey strips. Sprinkle with pomegranate seeds or granadilla pips. Stand back and admire your work. When ready to eat, pour over the salad dressing.

SUNSET SALAD DRESSING:

2 pieces ginger preserve
2 cloves garlic
½ cup sugar
1 cup fresh strawberries
½ cup orange juice (freshly squeezed or bottled)
¼ cup lemon juice (freshly squeezed or bottled)
¾ cup mayonnaise
½ cup vinegar
few drops hot chilli sauce
salt and pepper

Blend the ingredients until smooth.

SERVES 6–8

LEAF ME ALONE

'Desserts to dive for!'

divine
DESSERTS

non-dairy CREAMY VELVET ICE CREAM

WHEN I MAKE ICE CREAM, FOR THE SAME EFFORT, I MAKE A LARGE QUANTITY. THERE ARE SO MANY DIFFERENT ICE CREAMS AND PUDDINGS MADE FROM THIS BASIC RECIPE THAT YOU MAY AS WELL HAVE A FEW TUBS IN YOUR FREEZER!

**4 cups non-dairy creamer
(Rich's™ or Orley Whip™)
12 eggs
½ cup icing sugar (if you are
using Orley Whip™, add 1 cup)
1 tsp vanilla essence**

Beat the creamer in a large bowl until firm. Cream the eggs, icing sugar and vanilla essence very well in a food processor until light and creamy. Add the eggs and icing sugar to the creamer and beat until well combined.

Divide the mixture into four separate portions and pour into plastic containers. When a recipe calls for a portion of ice cream, it's one of these four portions.

Freeze until required.

1 PORTION SERVES 6–8

HEARD IT THROUGH THE GRAPEVINE

I ARRIVED HOME ONE EVENING TO FIND A BUNCH OF YOUNG MEN SITTING AROUND MY KITCHEN TABLE IN A VERY 'RELAXED' STATE OF MIND. THEY HAD FOUND MY PICKLED GRAPES! AND BY THE LOOK OF THINGS, THAT'S EXACTLY WHAT THEY WERE TOO – PICKLED!

**2 kg seedless red or
white grapes
2 cups vodka
2 cups Sprite Zero® or
ordinary Sprite®**

Remove all the stems from the grapes. Wash the grapes and pack into a large glass container with a tight fitting, rubber-sealed lid. Pour over the vodka and Sprite®, and leave to marinate for about three days before you try them.

SERVES 10–12

Sivan's
COOKIES-AND-CREAM ICE CREAM

I LOVE ENTERTAINING MY FRIENDS IN THE KITCHEN! THAT'S WHERE WE CHAT, LAUGH, TASTE AND SOMETIMES DRINK THE GLASS OF WINE THAT SHOULD HAVE GONE INTO THE FOOD! WE WERE SO BUSY DOING THAT ONE FRIDAY AFTERNOON THAT WE DIDN'T REALISE SHABBOS (SABBATH) WAS ABOUT TO COME IN AND, BECAUSE COOKING HAD TO STOP, THE BISCUITS IN THE OVEN HAD TO COME OUT! WHAT WAS I GOING TO DO WITH HALF-COOKED BISCUIT DOUGH? 'MIX IT WITH ICE CREAM AND MAKE COOKIES-AND-CREAM ICE CREAM MADE WITH HALF-COOKED DOUGH!' SUGGESTED MY FRIEND. AND SO IT WAS COOKIES-AND-CREAM ICE CREAM FOR DESSERT!

1 portion non-dairy creamy velvet ice cream (see page 195)

FOR THE COOKIE DOUGH
½ cup non-dairy margarine
1 cup brown sugar
1 egg
1 cup flour, sifted
1½ tsp baking powder
pinch salt

COOKIE DOUGH:

Preheat the oven to 200 °C. Cream the margarine, sugar and egg until fluffy. Add the flour, baking powder and salt to form a soft dough.

Press into a greased baking tray, spread about 5 mm thick, and bake for 7–10 minutes – no longer, as you don't want it to be crispy.

Remove from the oven and leave to cool. Break up into rough, bite-size pieces. Fold into the ice cream and freeze immediately.

TO SERVE:

Serve with fresh strawberries.

SERVES 6

CRISPY BANANA BLINTZES
with caramel pecan sauce

THE CRISPNESS OF THE PHYLLO PASTRY AND THE SOFTNESS OF THE BANANA MAKE THIS FRAGILE PARCEL SEEM SO VULNERABLE WITHOUT THE SECURITY OF ITS CARAMEL PECAN SAUCE. HOWEVER, BEFORE YOU ROLL IT UP AND COVER IT IN A BLANKET OF CARAMEL, REMEMBER THAT IT LIKES TO BE TUCKED IN WITH SOME ICE CREAM! GOOD NIGHT, EAT TIGHT!

8 bananas, peeled and cut in half widthwise

juice of 1 lemon

½ cup syrup dissolved in ½ cup boiling water

1 tsp ground cinnamon

1 x 500 g box phyllo pastry

FOR THE CARAMEL PECAN SAUCE

½ cup soft brown sugar

½ cup syrup

2 Tbsp non-dairy margarine

½ cup non-dairy creamer

pinch salt

100 g pecan nuts (crush the packet with a rolling pin to break the pecans)

Preheat the oven to 200 °C. Toss the bananas in the lemon juice, then discard the juice. Place the bananas in a medium-sized ovenproof dish, not too big as they should be covered in syrup. Drizzle with syrup and sprinkle with cinnamon.

Bake in the oven for 10 minutes, turn them over and leave to cook for a further 10 minutes until soft but not so mushy that they start to disintegrate! Depending on the ripeness, 10 minutes could be enough and they won't need to be turned over. Remove from the oven and set aside to cool.

While the bananas are baking, cut each phyllo sheet in quarters, and keep covered so they don't dry out.

Place a piece of baked banana on the top half of each piece of pastry, fold in the sides and roll up like a spring roll.

Place the blintzes onto a well-greased baking tray, spray with olive oil spray, sprinkle with cinnamon and sugar, and cover with clingfilm or foil. Place in the fridge until ready to bake.

When ready to serve, place in a preheated oven at 200 °C for a few minutes until golden brown. Drizzle with Caramel Pecan Sauce.

CARAMEL PECAN SAUCE:
Place all the ingredients (except the nuts) in a pot and bring to the boil, whisking continuously. It's important to whisk the sauce as the ingredients start to melt, as this prevents the sauce from separating.

Once it starts to boil, reduce the heat, add the nuts and continue to simmer for a minute or two. Remove from the heat and reheat when ready to serve with the blintzes, or serve at room temperature.

This can be made in advance and reheated just before serving.

MAKES 16

GRANNY APPLES' CAKE
with hot syrup and custard sauce

GRANNY APPLES WAS THE MATRIARCH OF THE FAMILY AND MY BELOVED GREAT AUNT. AS HER SURNAME WAS SMITH, HER GRANDCHILDREN AFFECTIONATELY CALLED HER 'GRANNY APPLES' RATHER THAN GRANNY SMITH! SO TO MY DEAR AUNTY RINA, THIS ONE'S FOR YOU.

½ cup non-dairy margarine
1 cup sugar
3 eggs
1 cup flour
2 tsp baking powder
pinch salt
½ cup water
1 x 765 g tin pie apples
1 tsp ground cinnamon
½ cup raisins (optional)

FOR THE SYRUP
1 cup water
1 cup sugar
½ cup non-dairy margarine
1 tsp vanilla essence
½ cup non-dairy creamer
½ cup chopped walnuts
(optional)

FOR THE CUSTARD SAUCE
1 cup non-dairy creamer
1 cup water
3 egg yolks
1 Tbsp brandy (optional)
1 tsp vanilla essence
1 heaped Tbsp custard powder

Preheat the oven to 180 °C. Cream the margarine and sugar until light and fluffy. Add the eggs and continue to beat. Add the dry ingredients and the water.

Pour half of the mixture into a lightly greased oblong pie dish. Arrange the apples on top of the cake mixture and sprinkle with cinnamon and raisins. Pour over the other half of the cake mixture.

Bake for 45–50 minutes. After 35 minutes, prepare the syrup.

SYRUP:

Pour the water into a pot, add the sugar and bring to the boil. Turn the heat down and leave to simmer for 5 minutes. Once the sugar has dissolved, remove from the heat.

Immediately add the margarine and vanilla, and allow it to melt, stirring gently. Add the non-dairy creamer and whisk well together. Add the chopped walnuts.

The cake should now be ready to be removed from the oven. Pour the syrup over the cake as it comes out of the oven.

Serve with custard sauce.

CUSTARD SAUCE:

Mix all the ingredients in a bowl and transfer to a double boiler. Allow the mixture to thicken, then remove from the heat and pour into a pouring jug. Place clingfilm over the top of the custard – this helps prevent a 'custard carpet' from forming.

Note: My aunt never added walnuts because Uncle Morris always complained that they got stuck under his plate! But the younger members of the family with strong 'tzeina' (teeth) like it a little nutty!

SERVES 10–12

199 |

HAZELNUTTA

THIS IS THE PERFECT 'I'VE GOT TO IMPRESS THEM' DESSERT! TWO LAYERS OF HAZELNUT MERINGUE PROTECTING A THICK VELVETY LAYER OF HAZELNUT ICE CREAM. TO PUT THE DECORATIVE FINISHING TOUCHES TO THIS DESSERT, USE THE IDEAS FROM THE CHOCOLATE ROLLER COASTERS RECIPE ON PAGE 211. THAT SHOULD SEAL IT FOR YOU!

6 eggs, separated
1 cup sugar
200 g hazelnuts, roughly crushed
with a rolling pin
½ cup icing sugar
2 cups non-dairy creamer
1 x 250 g bottle Pralinutta Duo™
(duo chocolate spread available
at most supermarkets)
cocoa powder for dusting

Before you start this recipe, decide on the size of your springform tin. Place the base of the tin onto baking paper and trace it twice as you need a meringue bottom and a lid for this pudding.

Beat the egg whites until stiff, then gradually add the sugar and continue beating until a smooth consistency is achieved, just like soft-serve ice cream – parev of course! Fold in the nuts and divide the mixture into two portions. Spread over the two outlined bases on the baking paper. Keep within the lines (about 5 mm) as the meringue does swell a little while baking. Rather spread the mixture higher than wider. Bake at 120 °C for 1½ –2 hours.

Meanwhile beat the egg yolks and icing sugar until light and creamy. Beat the non-dairy creamer until firm, then slowly add the egg yolk mixture, beating as you do.

Place the bottle of chocolate spread in a bowl of boiling water for about 1 minute to soften a little. Add half of the chocolate spread to the cream mixture and mix well. Place into the fridge until the meringues are ready.

Remove the meringues from the oven, peel off the paper and place one layer into the bottom of the springform tin directly onto the base. If it's a little too big for the tin, shave it slightly on the sides with a knife so that it fits in snugly.

Pour the rest of the chocolate spread over the meringue base, followed by the cream mixture. At this point cover the meringue base and cream mixture with foil and freeze. Place the second meringue layer in an airtight container and cover with foil until ready to serve. (It will keep for 3–4 weeks.)

When ready to serve, release the meringue and ice cream onto a plate, and place the second meringue layer on top. To serve dust with cocoa or decorate with some of your favourite chocolate creations.

SERVES 8–10

warm, sticky
CHOCOLATE MOUSSE CAKE

THIS IS ABSOLUTELY DIVINE, ABSOLUTELY SIMPLE, AND ABSOLUTELY GESHMAK!

1 x 400 g packet chocolate cake mix (Moir's™ is kosher)
150 g dark, non-dairy chocolate
2 cups boiling water

Preheat the oven to 180 °C. Make the chocolate cake according to the directions on the box, using water or soya milk instead of milk. Pour into a well-greased, round ovenproof dish.

The cake mixture should not go more than halfway up the sides of the dish, as the melted chocolate liquid still has to be poured over the cake batter before baking.

Melt the chocolate in the boiling water. Pour the chocolate liquid evenly over the cake batter and bake for 45 minutes.

It will still look uncooked and soft on the top, but this is a self-basting pudding (makes its own sauce) and needs to have this sauce.

Serve warm with vanilla ice cream.

SERVES 8–10

hot, oozy squoozy
ICED CINNAMON BUNS

THIS RECIPE HELPED A FRIEND OF MINE GET OVER HER YEAST PHOBIA. SHE JUST COULDN'T WAIT FOR ME TO MAKE THEM AGAIN, WHICH FORCED HER TO DO IT. HALF THE FUN OF MAKING THESE CINNAMON BUNS IS NOT ONLY EATING THEM WHILE THEY'RE STILL HOT, BUT ENJOYING THE AROMA THAT PERMEATES THE WHOLE HOUSE WHILE THEY'RE BAKING! THAT AROMA CAN NEVER BE CAPTURED IN A BOTTLE, NO MATTER HOW HARD THE 'SMELLIES' MARKET HAS TRIED.

FOR THE DOUGH
½ cup non-dairy margarine
1 cup non-dairy creamer
2 cups water
1 tsp vanilla
½ cup sugar
6 cups sifted flour
1 x 85 g packet non-dairy
vanilla pudding
2 x 10 g packets dry yeast
(rapid rising)
2 eggs, lightly beaten
1 tsp salt

FOR THE FILLING
½ cup soft non-dairy margarine
1 cup brown sugar
2 tsp ground cinnamon
raisins (optional)

FOR THE ICING
2 Tbsp melted non-dairy
margarine
2 Tbsp boiling water
1 tsp lemon juice
2 cups icing sugar, sifted

DOUGH:

Place the margarine, non-dairy creamer, water, vanilla and sugar into a saucepan and heat until the margarine has melted. Do not boil.

Remove from the heat and set aside to cool, but it should still be slightly warm when you add it to the dry ingredients.

Place the flour into a large bowl. Make a well in the centre and add the rest of the ingredients in the following order: the vanilla pudding, yeast, warm melted margarine mixture, eggs and salt.

With a wooden spoon slowly incorporate the dry ingredients by drawing the flour from the sides into the warm liquid. When it becomes difficult to use the spoon, start kneading the dough with your hands until it is reasonably well combined.

This is the best arm exercise in town! Make enough cinnamon buns and you can wave those flappy arms goodbye.

Empty the dough out onto a lightly floured board and continue kneading until a smooth, elastic consistency is achieved where the dough doesn't stick to your fingers and has a lovely 'dough sheen' to it.

Cover the bowl with plastic that has been lightly oiled on the side that comes into contact with the dough. Leave the dough to double in size. This should take 30–45 minutes.

Knead the dough down to its original size. Divide the dough in two and roll out each half into a rectangular shape on a lightly floured surface.

FILLING:

Spread half the margarine onto one half of the dough, sprinkle with half the brown sugar and cinnamon, and then add the raisins.

Roll the dough up and cut it into 3 cm wide pieces. They will still rise quite a bit. Do the same with the other piece of dough.

The buns can either be baked in a well-greased muffin tin or in a rectangular ovenproof dish. Don't put them too close to one another, as they need a little 'breathing space'. Cover and leave them to double in size again. Bake at 180 °C for 20 minutes or until golden brown.

ICING:

While the buns are baking, prepare the icing as the buns need to be covered as soon as they come out of the oven!

If you made the icing earlier, add a few drops of boiling water to soften it again.

Melt the margarine in the boiling water, either on the stove or in the microwave.

Add the lemon juice, then slowly start adding the sifted icing sugar, stirring continuously until a nice smooth paste starts to form (it should be slightly softer than toothpaste). You may need to add a little more boiling water as you go along to acquire this consistency.

Using a spatula or spoon, spread a helping of icing over each bun, ensuring that the entire bun is coated with a thin layer, before moving on to the next one. The icing should melt into the bun immediately.

If they've already cooled down, pop them into the microwave for a few seconds, one or two at a time. In this way you will have better control over them because a second or two too long in a microwave can ruin anything.

MAKES 18–20

CAPPUCCINO
chino

THIS PUDDING DOES TWO THINGS – IT ALLOWS YOU THE OPPORTUNITY TO EXPERIENCE A NON-DAIRY ALTERNATIVE TO TIRAMISU, AND GIVES YOU THE OPPORTUNITY TO END YOUR MEAL WITH 'A CREAMY COFFEE EXPERIENCE', RATHER THAN A CUP OF BLACK COFFEE.

5 large eggs
1 tsp vanilla essence
3 Tbsp icing sugar
3 cups non-dairy creamer
½ cup coffee liqueur
1 Tbsp coffee powder, dissolved
in 1 cup boiling water
2 boxes Boudoir™
(finger) biscuits
1 x 250 ml bottle non-dairy
chocolate sauce (All Joy®
is non-dairy)
cocoa powder for dusting

Beat the eggs, vanilla and icing sugar until light and creamy.

In a separate bowl, beat the cream until firm. Combine the egg mixture and cream, and beat well.

Place one-third of the cream mixture into the bottom of a rectangular glass or ceramic dish (35 x 25 x 6 cm), and spread it out to line the base. (This pudding can also be made in individual cups or small bowls.)

Combine the coffee liqueur with the black coffee.

Dip each finger biscuit into the coffee mixture and place a whole packet of dipped biscuits on top of the first cream layer. Zigzag a generous layer of chocolate sauce over the biscuits.

Place another layer of the cream mixture over the biscuits, followed by another layer of biscuits, chocolate sauce and finally the last layer of cream.

Peak the cream with the back of a spoon to make it look like 'a windy day at sea' and dust with cocoa powder.

Freeze immediately.

SERVES 10–12

206 | DIVINE DESSERTS

waste-not-want-not
HOT CINNAMON PUDDING

OR 'RECYCLED CHALLAH AND BABKE', AS MY SONS CALL IT! WELL, THERE'S NO WAY I'M WASTING ONE PIECE OF CHALLAH AFTER STANDING AND KNEADING, SEPARATING, PLAITING, RISING AND BAKING IT! SO, IT'S INTO THIS VARIATION OF BREAD-AND-BUTTER PUDDING THAT IT GOES!

1 challah (plain, with no poppy or sesame seeds) or 1 babke, or whatever's left over to make up a loaf
½ cup apricot jam
non-dairy margarine for greasing
2 tsp ground cinnamon
1 cup brown sugar
2 cups raisins

FOR THE CUSTARD
1½ cups non-dairy creamer
1½ –2 cups water
3 egg yolks + 2 eggs (extra large)
1 tsp vanilla essence

Remove the crust from the base, sides, ends and top of the challah or babke. Try to remove as much excess crust as you can, although the plaiting does make this a little tricky.

Cut the bread into 1 cm slices and spread each slice with jam.

Grease a deep square ovenproof dish with non-dairy margarine. Place the first layer of bread in the dish. Sprinkle with cinnamon and sugar, and then a handful of raisins.

Repeat the layers of bread with jam and toppings until all the bread has been used.

The challah should only half fill the dish, as it will absorb the custard mixture and rise quite a bit.

CUSTARD:
Make up the custard mixture by combining all the ingredients in a bowl. Pour it over the bread and press down with the back of a spoon so that the bread absorbs the liquid.

The challah should be completely covered by the custard mixture with a little extra floating on top for extra absorption while standing.

Cover and leave to stand for at least 1 hour (place in the fridge on a hot day). It can be frozen at this point if you are not going to serve it that day. They freeze well. Only bake when the pudding is going to be served.

Preheat the oven to 200 °C and bake for 25–30 minutes or until golden on top. There's no need to test with a skewer, as the pudding must be moist. Don't put it onto a hot plate or leave it in a warming oven, as this will dry it out! I usually bake mine as we're sitting down to eat the first course. Serve with creamy velvet ice cream (see page 195) or custard sauce (see page 199).

SERVES 8–10

chill out
CHEESECAKE

I'VE ALWAYS SAID THAT THERE'S A NON-DAIRY OPTION FOR MOST DAIRY PRODUCTS AND, IF THERE ISN'T AN ALTERNATIVE, YOU CAN LIVE WITHOUT IT OR YOU DON'T NEED IT ANYWAY. HOWEVER, THERE COULD BE ONE EXCEPTION FOR SOME AND THAT'S CHEESECAKE. BUT THEN AGAIN I SAY, 'CAN WE LIVE WITHOUT IT OR DO WE NEED IT?' HOWEVER, I'LL STICK TO MY WORD AND GIVE YOU A NON-DAIRY ALTERNATIVE. THE CHOICE, OF COURSE, IS YOURS!

2 eggs
½ cup sugar
⅓ cup fresh lemon juice
1 cup non-dairy creamer
¾ cup cold water
1 x 85 g packet non-dairy vanilla pudding
1 x 85 g packet lemon jelly
1 cup boiling water
½ cup cold water
1 box Boudoir™ (finger) biscuits
icing sugar for dusting
sliced strawberries and mint leaves to garnish

Cream the eggs, sugar and lemon juice together until light and creamy.

Place the non-dairy creamer, cold water and vanilla pudding into a bowl and beat until firm.

Dissolve the lemon jelly in the boiling water then add the ½ cup cold water.

Immediately dip the finger biscuits into the jelly (before it starts to set!) and line a glass or freezer-safe pie dish with the biscuits. Dip all the biscuits. If there are any left over after you have lined the base, set them aside on a plate to be used as a second layer.

Once you've dipped all the biscuits, immediately pour the remaining jelly liquid through a strainer into the bowl with the cream mixture, then beat again until well combined.

Pour half the cream mixture over the biscuit base, arrange another layer of biscuits on top (if there are any left), and add the other half of the cream mixture.

Place in the freezer. When ready to serve, remove the pudding from the freezer, dust with icing sugar, and decorate with sliced strawberries and mint leaves.

SERVES 8–12

chocolate
ROLLER COASTERS

THESE ARE SIMPLE, EFFECTIVE AND DECORATIVE, AND JUST LOOK DIFFERENT! PEOPLE DON'T EXPECT THE COASTER BENEATH THEIR LONG-STEMMED DESSERT GLASSES TO BE EDIBLE! THEY CAN, OF COURSE, ALSO BE USED TO DECORATE THE TOP OF A DESSERT. THERE ARE MANY DIFFERENT DESIGNS YOU CAN CREATE, MAKING THEM UNIQUE FOR EVERY OCCASION. I MAKE THEM UP IN BATCHES AND FREEZE THEM.

**300 g dark chocolate (I use
2 slabs Orley™)
baking paper (about 0.5 m)
5 ml syringe (discard the needle)**

Melt the chocolate in a glass or stainless steel bowl over boiling water or in a double boiler. Place the baking paper on a flat surface.
Draw the melted chocolate up into the syringe and create your own design by slowly pressing the chocolate out of the syringe and onto the paper. When drawing up the chocolate into the syringe, tilt the bowl to get more depth to the chocolate, which will prevent air bubbles from getting into it. Instead of a syringe, you could use a Ziploc™ bag with a tiny hole cut in one of the corners.

DESIGN IDEAS:

- You can also use non-dairy white chocolate. However, when using two colours, make sure the first layer sets completely before adding the next.
- Make a Star of David for a Jewish Holiday or Shabbat.
- Create simple flowers, geometric designs, hearts, lattice designs and spirals, or if you're nervous doing it free hand, use stencils available from art and kitchen stores.

These really are fun and do look special!

MAKES ±18

apple and cinnamon
CALMING COMPOTE

TODAY RELAXATION AND MANAGING OUR STRESS LEVELS HAVE BECOME AN INTEGRAL PART OF OUR LIFESTYLE. WITH THE HELP OF WIND CHIMES, SOOTHING MUSIC AND RUNNING WATER WE CAN ALMOST BE TRANSPORTED TO AN IDYLLIC PIECE OF PARADISE. FOR SOME THIS IS WONDERFUL AND IT WORKS, BUT IF YOU'RE ANYTHING LIKE MY FAMILY, YOU'LL START GETTING HUNGRY BEFORE THE JOURNEY HAS EVEN BEGUN! WHAT BETTER WAY TO EMBARK ON YOUR SPIRITUAL ROAD TO RECOVERY THAN WITH A BOWL OF CALMING COMPOTE! THIS CAN BE SERVED EITHER ICE COLD IN SUMMER OR WARM IN WINTER!

3 apple and cinnamon tea bags (Twinings®)
4 cups boiling water
1 cup sultanas
500 g frozen berries
1 x 410 g tin mango slices, drained and cut into smaller pieces
18 litchis, pips removed (when in season)
1 Tbsp custard powder mixed with ¼ cup cold water

Allow the tea bags to draw in the boiling water for about 20 minutes. Stir every now and then. Remove the bags and pour the tea into a pot.

Add the sultanas, berries, mangoes and litchis, and bring to the boil. As it just starts to boil, add the custard mixture to the fruit. Stir and leave it to thicken for a minute or two, then remove from the heat.

SERVES 8–10

pineapple and GARDEN MINT GRANITA

A FRIEND'S DAUGHTER TOOK HER 'GAP YEAR' IN LONDON AND WORKED AS A WAITRESS IN A PUB. AFTER SEEING FRESH MINT GROWING IN ABUNDANCE IN MY GARDEN, SHE DECIDED IT WAS TIME TO CUT BACK THE BUSHES AND CREATE ONE OF HER FAMOUS MINTY COCKTAILS. I MUST ADMIT IT'S VERY REFRESHING AFTER ROAST BEEF AND YORKSHIRE PUDDING!

¼ cup water
juice of 1 lemon
¾ cup sugar
2 pineapples
2 Tbsp chopped fresh mint
½ cup vodka (optional)

Boil together the water, lemon juice and sugar until the sugar dissolves completely.

While this is boiling, cut the pineapples into chunks and blend, together with the mint, in a food processor or liquidiser until smooth.

Add the sugar water to the pineapple and mint, and blend for a few more seconds.

Pour into a glass bowl and freeze for about 3 hours. Remove the granita from the freezer, break it up and place it in the food processor again, together with the vodka. Blend until smooth, then refreeze.

Remove from the freezer about 30 minutes before serving to soften a little.

SERVES 6–8

summer breeze
TROPICAL FREEZE

WINTER OR SUMMER, THE BEST PART OF MAKING THIS FREEZE IS THAT IT IS AN ABSOLUTE BREEZE!

**2 Tbsp freshly squeezed
lemon juice
1 cup fresh orange juice (bottled)
1 cup guava juice (bottled)
1 x 410 g tin mango slices
½ cup sugar
1 x 85 g packet strawberry jelly
1 large pineapple, cut
into chunks
500 g frozen berries**

Pour the lemon juice, orange juice, guava juice, the liquid from the tinned mangoes and sugar into a pot and bring to the boil. Switch off the heat as it starts to boil. Dissolve the strawberry jelly in ½ cup cold water, ensuring that it is completely dissolved. Add the strawberry jelly to the juice and mix well with a whisk.

Place the pineapple, berries and drained mangoes into a food processor, and pulse a few times.

Slowly add the fruit juice and jelly mixture, and blend until smooth.

Pour through a strainer into the container in which it will be frozen. Place in the freezer for 3–4 hours. Remove from the freezer and mash it with a potato masher or fork to prevent it from separating.

Put it back into the freezer and freeze until required. It doesn't have to be completely smooth when you refreeze it; a little texture is fine.

TO SERVE:

I normally freeze mine in a square or rectangular container as it makes for easier scraping into individual bowls.

You could also scoop out balls and build a mound. Decorate with mint and refreeze until needed.

SERVES 12

Eden's ROCKY ROAD CHOCOLATE CLUSTERS

MY DAUGHTER EDEN LOVES THE KITCHEN AND TOGETHER WITH HER COUSIN HANNAH THEY COOK UP A TORNADO, NEVER MIND A STORM. WHEN THEY SEE THE SHOCK ON MY FACE THEY ALWAYS SAY THE SAME THING, 'IT WASN'T ME'. MUST BE SOMETHING IN THAT STATEMENT FOR SHAGGY TO HAVE WRITTEN A WHOLE SONG ABOUT IT. WE'RE ALWAYS LOOKING FOR NEW FOOD IDEAS FOR MY SON WHO IS NOT ONLY MILK BUT GLUTEN INTOLERANT AS WELL. SO FAR, THIS HAS BEEN ONE OF HER BETTER CREATIONS.

2 x 150 g slabs Orley™ non-dairy dark chocolate
1 cup raw peanuts
1 cup roughly chopped marshmallows
½ cup desiccated coconut
2 cups cornflakes
±10 red glacé cherries
±10 green glacé cherries
1 x 100 g packet honeycomb

Melt the chocolate in a large bowl over boiling water or in a double boiler.

Add the rest of the ingredients and combine well so that everything is coated in chocolate.

Line a baking tray with baking paper and pour the chocolate mixture onto the tray.

Press it down with the back of a spoon, but not too firmly. Let it remain a little uneven, then allow it to set in the fridge.

Cut into small squares when cold, and keep in the freezer. Alternatively, serve the clusters in gold or silver foil cookie cups.

SERVES ENOUGH! IT WAS OUR DAUGHTER'S BATMITZVAH, AND FOR THE FUNCTION I HAD SASHES APPROPRIATELY EMBROIDERED FOR ALL THE WAITERS. WHEN I PHONED THE CATERER TO ASK HOW MANY WAITERS THERE WOULD BE, HE SIMPLY ANSWERED 'ENOUGH', AND DOWN WENT THE TELEPHONE. I HAD TO INCLUDE THAT LITTLE STORY HERE BECAUSE THAT'S EXACTLY HOW MANY THIS RECIPE WILL SERVE – ENOUGH! YOU WON'T RUN OUT. DID I HAVE ENOUGH SASHES? NO!

peanut buttercup
FUDGE ICE CREAM

THIS IS A DELICIOUS FUDGE SAUCE TO 'MARBLE' THROUGH ICE CREAM. BUT IT SHOULD NOT ONLY BE SWIRLED THROUGH, SO I'VE BEEN TOLD. THE ICE CREAM NEEDS TO BE SMOTHERED IN THE SAUCE AS WELL!

FOR THE FUDGE SAUCE
1 cup non-dairy creamer
1 cup water
¾ cup peanut butter
1 cup syrup
1 cup caramel chocolate chips
2 x 150 g slabs Orley™
non-dairy dark chocolate

FOR THE ICE CREAM
2 portions creamy velvet
ice cream (see page 195)

FUDGE SAUCE:
Combine all the ingredients and melt in a double boiler or in the microwave.

ICE CREAM:
Place one slightly softened portion of ice cream into a glass bowl. Spoon half of the cooled fudge sauce over the first layer of ice cream. Cover the sauce with the other portion of softened ice cream.

Use a knife and zigzag the fudge sauce through the ice cream as you would with a marble cake. Place in the freezer. Place the other half of the sauce into a container and freeze.

When ready to serve the ice cream, reheat the other half of the sauce and pour over the ice cream as you would chocolate sauce. If you find that the sauce is a bit too thick, add a little non-dairy creamer mixed with a little water.

SERVES 6–8

INDEX

Page numbers in bold indicate photographs.